The Getaway Guide
to the American Southwest

Books By Richard Harris

2 to 22 Days in the American Southwest
2 to 22 Days in the Pacific Northwest
2 to 22 Days in Texas
2 to 22 Days in Florida
Unique California
Unique Oregon
American Southwest TravelSmart Trip Planner
Hidden Southwest
The Maya Route/La Ruta Maya (with Stacy Ritz)
Santa Fe and Beyond (with Roger Rapoport)
Hidden Rockies (with John Gottberg)
Choose the Northwest (with John Howells)
The New Key to Cancún and the Yucatán
Hidden Colorado
Hidden New Mexico
National Trust Guide: Santa Fe
The New Key to Guatemala
Hidden Bahamas
Hidden Baja
Hidden Cancún and the Yucatán
Hidden Guatemala
AAA Hidden Highways of
Northern California (with Ray Riegert)
Hidden Highways of Arizona

Website: home.earthlink.net/~richardkharris

The Getaway Guide
to the American Southwest

Richard Harris

RDR Books
Oakland, California

Getaway Guide to the American Southwest

RDR Books
4456 Piedmont
Oakland, CA 94611
Phone: (510) 595-0595
Fax: (510) 595-0598
E-mail: read@rdrbooks.com
Website: www.rdrbooks.com

ISBN: 1-57143-073-3

Library of Congress Catalog Card Number 2001095662

Editors: Bob Drews, Kim Klescewski, Sayre Van Young
Proofreader: Joanna Pearlman
Cover Photograph: Dewitt Jones
Cover Design: Jennifer Braham
Text Design: Paula Morrison
Researcher: Bryan Knapp
Production: Sonia Alix

Distributed in Canada by General Distribution Service
325 Humber College Boulevard, Toronto, ON M9W7C3

Distributed in England and Europe by Airlift Book Company
8 The Arena, Mollison Avenue, Enfield, Middlesex, England
EN37NJ

Distributed in Australia and New Zealand by Astam Books Pty Ltd.
57-61 John Street, Liechardt, New South Wales 2038

Printed in Canada by Transcontinental Printing

Contents

Author's Note

Although the author has made every effort to ensure accuracy, readers are advised to inquire locally, particularly regarding museum/attraction hours and routings, which are subject to change. We suggest readers supplement this book with current local maps. Prices mentioned in the book are approximate and subject to change. Because the least expensive rooms tend to be booked first, you may be asked to pay more than the minimum rates quoted. A number of the roads that form part of this itinerary are mountainous and in a few cases not suitable for oversize or recreational vehicles. You should carry chains in the mountains during the winter months and be prepared for sudden storms that can block access during other times of the year. Check the weather forecast before setting out into remote or mountainous areas. Comments or suggestions e-mailed to the author at RichardKHarris@earthlink.net or sent snail-mail care of the publisher are welcome.

How to Use This Book

Under the ancient volcano in northern New Mexico lives the nation's largest community of nuclear physicists. Twelve miles to the east, the people of San Ildefonso Pueblo speak their Native American language, dance in time-honored ceremonies, and make pottery by methods a thousand years old. Five miles to the south, in the Bandelier wilderness, you can walk for three days without coming to a road.

Welcome to the American Southwest, where pristine wilderness and civilizations many centuries old endure side by side with particle physics. *Getaway Guide to the American Southwest* contains a self-guided travel itinerary for a three-week road trip that will take you to the most fascinating places in New Mexico, Arizona, and the southern parts of Colorado, Utah, and Nevada. The tour follows a 3,000-mile meandering loop, mostly on less-used secondary highways. It intersects Interstate 40 several times and connects with Interstates 15, 25, and 70, so it's easy to join and leave from any direction.

If you have less than three weeks to explore, use any of the route's various segments as a relaxing scenic alternative to Interstate 40. These segments range from a few hours to a week or more. The tour takes you to eight national parks, thirteen national monuments, and assorted state parks, national forests, and Bureau of Land Management scenic areas. You'll also visit the lands of the Pueblo, Hopi, Zuñi, Navajo, and other indigenous people. At opposite poles of this South-western odyssey you'll find two of America's most unusual—even improbable—cities, Las Vegas and Santa Fe.

The itinerary format in this book is divided into 22 daily sections, containing:

1. A suggested schedule for each day's travel and sight-seeing.

2. A detailed travel route description for each driving segment of your trip.

3. Descriptive overviews and sightseeing highlights.

4. A suggested campground for each night of the trip, as well as restaurant and lodging recommendations for those who choose not to camp.

5. Tips on hiking, biking, and other outdoor recreation.

6. Itinerary options—excursion suggestions for travelers who have extra time.

7. User-friendly maps designed to show you what the road up ahead is really like.

Why 22 Days?

You wouldn't dream of touring Europe or India in less than three weeks, because you may have only that single chance to experience what you'll remember for the rest of your life. I invite you to explore America with the same "once in a lifetime" enthusiasm. You can see the Southwest in three weeks for just slightly more money than you'd spend if you stayed home, and the experience will rival any foreign vacation.

Recently I commented to a ranger on the surprising

number of European tourists visiting the national park where he worked. "You bet," he agreed. "Germans know a lot more about this part of the country than most Americans do."

My experience verified this as I recalled working my way through college as a Pikes Peak tour guide. Every week, tourists from east of the Mississippi, where states are smaller, would tell me their trip plans: go up Pikes Peak this morning, drive on and see the Grand Canyon this afternoon, spend the night in Vegas (tomorrow it's on to Disneyland). Twelve hours in the American Southwest. Maybe some of them accomplished it, too, back when many western highways had no speed limits. It's just that they didn't see very much.

The Southwest is vast. Distance isolates. The isolation protects ancient Native American traditions and Spanish colonial heritage. Some parts of the region remain completely uninhabited. There are roadless areas larger than some eastern states. The same vastness that makes the Southwest so alluring can isolate you behind a windshield, watching those green and white interstate signs that all look the same from coast to coast—except that out here they beckon to strange-sounding places like "Ácoma Sky City," "Shungo-pavi," and "Zyzyx Road." The heartland of the American Southwest ranks among the most wild and exotic places on earth. Take time to explore!

You don't even need a passport.

How Much Will It Cost?

I've taken this 22-day trip with a friend, in comfort, driving a Toyota Dolphin mini motor home, on a $2,200 trip budget, eating at restaurants twice a day, and returned home with eight new pieces of Indian jewelry and $21 in cash.

The major expense of the trip is gasoline. Figure 3,000 miles plus the round-trip driving distance from your home to the most convenient point on the tour route, at however many miles per gallon your rig or rental car gets.

If you cook your own meals, they'll cost the same as you'd spend eating at home. If you prefer the convenience of eating out, allow $9 to $15 per person per meal. There are only a handful of towns on this 22-day trip where you can find a more expensive restaurant if you want one.

I have tried to include lodging suggestions in all price ranges when possible. In some places along this route, there are no budget motels; in other places, there are no expensive ones. If you plan to take this trip without ever camping out, budget an average of $50 per night for lodging.

Public campground fees average around $12 per night, plus a couple of dollars extra if you want electric and water hookups. National forests and Arizona and New Mexico state parks charge anywhere from $7 to $17, depending on location and improvements; Utah state parks range from free to $11. Most national parks and monuments charge $10 to camp, plus the admission charge, though some campgrounds at the Grand Canyon charge up to $20. There are also abundant possibilities for free camping along national forest back roads.

Admission to state parks, national monuments, and national parks can range from an average of $5 per vehicle to a whopping $20 at the Grand Canyon. A $50 annual National Parks Pass, admitting you to all U.S. national parks and monuments free, is a sound investment on this trip. The pass also entitles you to take the fast lane and avoid long lines of cars at the South Rim of the Grand Canyon.

If you have funds to spare in your vacation budget, you can (1) buy American Indian jewelry, of which you'll see lots in all price ranges, and help out the nation's most impoverished ethnic minority; (2) take a chance at winning big in Las Vegas and keep trying until your money is used up; (3) take a chance at winning big in one of the Indian casinos found all over New Mexico, Arizona, and southwestern Colorado, thereby helping out the nation's most impoverished ethnic minority until your money is used up; or (4) forget about budgets and splurge on a great hotel or restaurant once in a while. You deserve it; this is your vacation.

When to Go

The best season for sightseeing in the Southwest is between May 1 and October 15. Before Memorial Day or after Labor Day, you can avoid crowds and extreme heat. Late spring travel reveals the desert in full bloom, while early autumn paints the mountainsides in aspen gold. However, summer travel gives you more hours of daylight, extra time to enjoy the desert at sunset and in the early morning.

Some destinations in this book, including the Grand Canyon North Rim, close in the winter. Most campgrounds are also closed. Sudden snowstorms can interrupt your trip at any point. Yet winter sports enthusiasts will discover fine ski slopes with remarkably short lift lines as well as excellent cross-country ski trails and plenty of sunshine.

Other places in the Southwest, such as Phoenix, Tucson,

and the Sonora Desert are left out of this itinerary simply because they're too hot to even consider visiting in the summer months. In winter, though, these areas are usually warm, dry, and pleasant.

The only impossibly hot place I've included in this itinerary is the Lower Colorado River area, from Las Vegas and Lake Mead down to Lake Havasu City. You can beat the midday 100° heat with indoor sightseeing in Las Vegas and Laughlin, or with a trip to the beach.

Transportation

Seeing the Southwest by train and bus is possible and enjoyable but restricting. You can get to the majority of places in this book only by private vehicle.

I recommend a camper truck, van conversion, or small motor home for this trip, but a sporty convertible or a station wagon full of kids will do fine. You won't need four-wheel drive, though you will sometimes find yourself driving on well-maintained unpaved roads. I've included only those roads where I've personally seen large RVs go. If you have a motor home the size of a Greyhound bus, you'll need a bit of hubris but not the AAA tow truck.

You can rent an RV, though it will cost more than all other expenses of your southwestern trip combined. If tight-budget travel is your plan, buy a tent instead. However, the luxury and comfort of motor home adventuring will cost no more than a student-style tour of Europe. It's particularly worth the extra cost if you're a newcomer to the world of RV travel and want to try one out on an extended trip before buying your own. Besides the hands-on experience, you can get ample advice about "rigs" from your neighbors in campgrounds everywhere. It's the ultimate icebreaker and a major topic of conversation.

RVs available for rent range in size from cramped to palatial. For this trip I suggest a modest size, preferably what is often called a "mini motor home," a custom-built living area mounted on a van-length frame. The places mentioned in this book can be reached even in a mammoth two-bedroom land yacht. Gas consumption will be alarming, and so will wear and tear on the driver's nerves. A big motor home is a wise choice, though, for families of four or more. It's true, you can sleep six in a mini motor home, but by Day 6 of this trip you may experience an almost overwhelming urge to leave the kids playing video games in a truck stop while you hop in your rig and high-tail it for the state line. Rental rates vary widely, from $300 to $500 per week for van-length RVs and from $500 to $800 per week for big motor homes. It pays to shop around.

Whatever vehicle you drive, be sure that it's sound enough to purr along through 3,000 miles of varied driving conditions including hot temperatures, high altitudes, and steep grades—or at least that you're equipped to handle roadside breakdowns when the nearest telephone or service station is 60 miles away. Be sure the spare tire and jack are in good condition, and carry a gallon of radiator coolant. For the confidence that comes from being ready for anything, take spare V-belts and radiator hoses as well as a basic automotive tool kit and an automotive repair manual.

Food and Lodging

Tent or RV, this itinerary assumes you're equipped to camp, at least part of the time. Fine hotels and restaurants are a big industry in some southwestern communities such as Santa Fe and Las Vegas, but for more than half of this trip, camping is the best way. On much of the route, food and lodging establishments are few, far between, and not luxurious.

My primary suggestion for each night is a public campground. When possible, I've picked campgrounds where the amenities include good rest rooms, evening walking trails, and slide shows by the campfire—all for a fraction of the cost of a room with TV at a ma-and-pa highway motel.

Anyone—casual tent camper, long-term motor home traveler, or seasoned backpacker—can develop a sudden yearning for a comfortable room with a hot shower and a telephone. This book describes alternate lodging suggestions that range from the basic necessities to big-splurge elegance. Tenderfoot noncampers can go the whole route without sleeping outdoors. When intriguing possibilities arise—bed and breakfasts, historic hotels, national park lodges, or casino hotels—I'll give you enough details so that you can make advance reservations. Otherwise, I'll direct you to the nearest town offering reasonably priced motels.

Nearby towns are also the place to find groceries or, if you must, a cheeseburger deluxe with fries or a Mexican combination plate. Where gourmet grocery shopping or local produce is available, I'll let you know. Sometimes regional food specialties make restaurant dining a vacation highlight; I'll show you the best places to find New Mexican green chile stew, Navajo fry bread, and Laughlin bargain breakfasts as well as sunny-side up eggs overlooking the Grand Canyon.

Recommended Reading

Getaway Guide to the American Southwest gives you the opportunity to see a kaleidoscope of cultures and wilderness panoramas. The more you know about them, the more you'll enjoy them. In this guide I only have space to tell you enough to whet your enthusiasm. New Mexico and Arizona have active regional publishers who put out hundreds of titles about the area, available in most New Mexico and Arizona bookstores. In addition, there are a number of perennial favorites, both fiction and nonfiction. Here are some of them:

The best book on the history and behind-the-scene workings of Las Vegas casino resorts is *The Money and the Power*, written by Santa Fe residents Roger Morris and Sally Denton.

Charles Lummis's vivid and evocative *The Land of Poco Tiempo*, written in 1893, contains descriptions of life among the Norteño, Pueblo, and Apache people which remain surprisingly accurate more than a century later. Also of interest is *The Delight Makers*, a novel of pre-historic Pueblo Indian life by Lummis's friend, archaeologist Adolph Bandelier.

Santa Fe's long, rich history is dramatized in a mini-Micheneresque saga entitled *The Centuries of Santa Fe* by Paul Horgan, lavish with accurate details on New Mexican life from early Spanish conquistadores to World

War II. Those interested in the early years of Santa Fe's Anglo artist colony will enjoy *Artists of the Canyons and Caminos* by Edna Robertson and Sarah Nestor.

Los Alamos' Manhattan Project and its impact on neighboring communities is the subject of Frank Waters's classic *The Woman at Otowi Bridge* as well as a recent popular thriller, *Stallion Gate*, by Martin Cruz Smith. Life in the Spanish villages of northern New Mexico is beautifully portrayed in *Bless Me, Ultima*, an autobiographical novel by retired University of New Mexico professor Rudolfo Anaya. Dr. Anaya's most recent book is *Alburquerque* (sic), a historical novel about New Mexico's largest city. For a broader, more offbeat view of the arrival of the twentieth century in northern New Mexico, read three big novels by Taos area author John Nichols: *The Milagro Beanfield War, The Magic Journey*, and *The Nirvana Blues*. The motion picture version of *The Milagro Beanfield War*, available on videocassette in both English and Spanish, may well be the best film portrayal ever of the people and problems of northern New Mexican villages.

Shelves full of books are available on the Navajo, from Navajo-English dictionaries to epic translations of Navajo song cycles. Good histories of the tribe include *The Navajo Nation* by Peter Iverson and the more readable *The Navajos* by Ruth M. Underhill and *The Book of the Navajo* by Raymond Friday Locke. Among several accounts of traditional Navajo life told to early-twentieth-century anthropologists, my favorite is *Son of Old Man Hat*, recorded in 1934 by National Research Council Fellow Walter Dyk.

Former President Clinton is among the growing number of fans of University of New Mexico journalism professor Tony Hillerman's unique whodunits about the Navajo Tribal Police which have been hot sellers in southwestern bookstores for many years. Among them are *The Eagle's Gift, The Fallen Man, Sacred Clowns, Talking God*, and *Coyote Waits*, as well as *The Dark Wind*, which producer Robert Redford made into a 1993 film starring Lou Diamond Phillips as Officer Jim Chee.

If I had to choose just one book for spare-time reading on this tour, it would be *Desert Solitaire*, the late Edward Abbey's memoir of a season as a ranger in Arches National Monument during the late 1950s. This collage of nature lore, environmental politics, and wilderness adventure is set in Moab, Arches, Canyonlands, Lake Powell, Capitol Reef, the Grand Canyon, and Supai. Abbey's novel, *The Monkey Wrench Gang*, a cult classic among environmental activists, inspired the popular southwestern pastime of "wrenching" (defending the environment by sabotage). Abbey's last novel, published in 1990, was a sequel to *The Monkey Wrench Gang* entitled *Hayduke Lives!*

The Exploration of the Colorado River and Its Canyons by Maj. John Wesley Powell is a record of the first expedition (1869) by river through the Grand Canyon—using wooden boats. Other enjoyable Grand Canyon classics include Joseph Wood Krutch's *Grand Canyon* and Colin Fletcher's *The Man Who Walked Through Time*.

Itinerary

Where to Start

Getaway Guide to the American Southwest is a loop trip. You can start anywhere on the circle.

For the majority of travelers, Las Vegas is the ideal starting point. It has the region's largest and busiest hub airport, and from most parts of the country it costs less to fly there than to Albuquerque, the other reasonable alternative. Motorists from the West Coast find Las Vegas easy to reach by interstate highway. Motorists coming from the East or Midwest may wish to start and end this itinerary at Albuquerque (Day 7), the junction of Inter-states 40 and 25.

Interstate Alternatives

For readers with less time and those en route to someplace else, segments of this tour can be adapted as relaxing scenic alternatives to Interstate 40, ranging from a few hours to more than a week:

• Between Albuquerque and Grants or Gallup, New Mexico, explore northern New Mexico, southern Colorado, and Anasazi country (Days 7 to 13).

• Between Gallup, New Mexico, and Kingman, Arizona (also intersecting I 70 at Green River, Utah, and I 15 at St. George, Utah), travel through the Navajo Reservations, Utah national parks, and Las Vegas (Days 15 to 22).

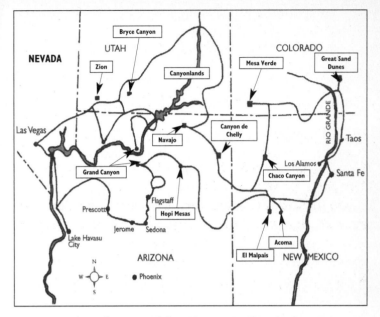

Grand Tour of the American Southwest

• Between Kingman and Flagstaff, Arizona, take a scenic detour through Prescott, Jerome, and Sedona (Day 3).

• Between Flagstaff and Holbrook, visit the Grand Canyon and Hopi mesas (Days 4 and 5).

• Between Holbrook, Arizona, and Grants, New Mexico, visit Petrified Forest National Park, the Zuñi Reservation, El Morro, and El Malpais (Day 6).

Sightseeing highlights you can see along I 40 without major detours are those in the Albuquerque/Santa Fe area (Days 7 and 8), the Grants area and Petrified Forest National Park (Day 7), and Flagstaff (Day 4).

It's also an easy 1-hour trip between Grants (Day 6) and Gallup (near Window Rock—Day 15), a useful shortcut for splitting this itinerary into two separate trips—a New Mexico tour and an around-the-Grand Canyon tour.

The itinerary in this book is flexible. Tailor it to fit your own time frame.

The Grand Tour of the American Southwest

DAY 1 Bright lights, noise, glitz, greed, and fast money round the clock—all with a unique theme-park veneer: experience the Las Vegas Strip.

DAY 2 Leaving the city, follow the Lake Mead shore to Hoover Dam. Swim and sunbathe at a desert beach. Then, following the Colorado River southward, visit the riverside fishing-and-gaming community of Laughlin, Nevada/ Bullhead City, Arizona, and see the London Bridge, improbably relocated to Lake Havasu City. Spend the night in Laughlin or continue to Kingman, where you can hike at Hualapai Mountain, an island of cool forest in the middle of the Mohave Desert.

DAY 3 Drive either fast, truck-packed I 40 or empty old Route 66 to Ash Fork, then turn south to loop through three unique central Arizona towns, each strikingly different from the others—Prescott, Jerome, and Sedona.

DAY 4 After a trip up scenic Oak Creek Canyon, explore Flagstaff. Within a few minutes' drive of the city limits, sightseeing highlights include Walnut Canyon National Monument, Lowell Observatory, and the Museum of Northern Arizona.

DAY 5 See Sunset Crater and Wupatki national monuments. Then take a long drive across the desert of the western Navajo Reservation to one of the most remote places in the United States, the ancient villages on top of the Hopi mesas.

DAY 6 Cross I 40 at Petrified Forest National Park, with its red, white, and blue painted desert. Then drive through the Zuñi Reservation to El Morro National Monument, the nation's first. Around Grants, New Mexico, visit El Malpais National Monument and Ácoma Pueblo on your way along the interstate to Albuquerque.

DAY 7 In Albuquerque, visit the Old Town Plaza and the region's best aquarium, then ride the tramway to the summit of Sandia Peak.

DAY 8 Drive the Turquoise Trail to Santa Fe, the capital of New Mexico for nearly four centuries. Visit the plaza and the plethora of great museums—and/or shop 'til you drop.

DAY 9 En route to Bandelier National Monument, visit Shidoni's sculpture garden, San Ildefonso Pueblo, and Los Alamos. Day-hike in Bandelier or explore by car higher in the Jemez Mountains. Spend a second night in Santa Fe, stay in Los Alamos, or continue to Taos.

DAY 10 Take the High Road to Taos through traditional Spanish villages, then descend into the Rio Grande Gorge. Spending the night in Taos, explore the town's unique cultural and artistic heritage.

DAY 11 Leaving Taos, continue north into Colorado to Great Sand Dunes National Park, the newest U.S. national park. Play among the sand dunes.

DAY 12 Drive to Durango, choosing either the direct route over Wolf Creek Pass or the less-traveled, even more scenic route through Cumbres and Chama.

DAY 13 Visit America's largest—and most popular—cliff dwellings at Mesa Verde National Park.

DAY 14 Today's trip takes you to two other 800-year-old Anasazi cities: Aztec Ruins and isolated Chaco Canyon, the largest pueblo city ever built.

DAY 15 Return from Chaco Canyon to I 40 near Gallup, New Mexico. Drive on to the Navajo Reservation, where you'll visit the Navajo Tribal Zoo and Hubbell Trading Post, ending the day at Canyon de Chelly.

DAY 16 Travel from Canyon de Chelly to Monument Valley, with an optional detour to Navajo National Monument, site of the Anasazi cliff dwellings, Betatakin and Keet Seel. At Monument Valley Tribal Park, visit traditional Navajo homes amid landscapes familiar from cowboy movies.

DAY 17 Heading into Utah, follow the Trail of the Ancients with a morning hiking break at Natural Bridges National Monument. Continue north to the town of Moab and Canyonlands National Park's Island in the Sky.

DAY 18 Three national parks in one day: awaken in Canyonlands and get an early start to tour Arches, then drive southwest, arriving at Capitol Reef in time to enjoy the cool of the evening in Utah's least-known national park.

DAY 19 From Capitol Reef to Bryce Canyon by way of the new Grand Staircase–Escalante National Monument, one of the most beautiful stretches of road on this tour, finally became part of a huge new national monument by presidential decree during the Clinton administration— more than 60 years after it was first nominated for national park status. End the day at busy Bryce Canyon National Park, where you can take an easy walk along the canyon rim or a more demanding one down among the hoodoos.

DAY 20 Take a scenic detour to Glen Canyon Dam and Lake Powell, then spend the night at Lee's Ferry, where the Grand Canyon begins.

DAY 21 Climax your vacation with a day and night on the North Rim of the Grand Canyon.

DAY 22 Travel from the Grand Canyon through Zion National Park, then take I 15 to Las Vegas, where your journey began three weeks ago.

Las Vegas

The gateway to the Southwest for motorists coming from the West Coast, as well as for anybody arriving by air, is Las Vegas. In a region characterized by timelessness, Las Vegas is one of the fastest-changing places in America. Its population growth rate is the highest in the nation, though its economy is based entirely on resorts and entertainment. Today, the Las Vegas metropolitan area has a population of over 1,300,000—more than half that of the entire state of Nevada. Its population has grown 384 percent since 1970.

Casino gambling was legalized in Nevada in 1931 under a plan to fund the state's public schools with gaming taxes. It remained the only state with legal casino gambling for six decades. El Rancho, the first casino resort on what is now the Strip, opened in 1941. But it was only after World War II, when Los Angeles (at a distance of 300 miles, the nearest city to Las Vegas) boomed, that casino development began in earnest. In 1946, "Bugsy" Siegel built the lavish Flamingo, reputedly with backing from organized crime figures who saw legalized casino gambling as a promising way to launder illegal profits.

The rumor seemed to be confirmed when, six months later, Siegel was shot and killed by hit men in his Hollywood home. Despite Las Vegas's gangster mystique, however, most casinos have never had any organized crime connections; the Flamingo is now owned by the Hilton chain.

To the north of Las Vegas is the U.S. Nuclear Testing Site. The first nuclear weapon atmospheric tests were conducted here in 1951, and each test became a local event as picnickers gathered to see the mushroom cloud 75 miles away. Six years later, the nuclear tests were moved underground, much to the disappointment of spectators. But by that time casino hotels were presenting new spectacles to entertain the booming numbers of visitors. Nightclub-style stage shows reached a level of opulence never seen before. Entertainers like Frank Sinatra, Jackie Gleason, and Liberace became synonymous with Las Vegas, as did Elvis Presley, Neil Diamond, and Wayne Newton in the years that followed.

In those days, everything in town was designed to encourage gambling. Psychological consultants were hired to select garish room decor designed to keep guests from spending too much time there. Then, in the late '70s, resort operators became aware that some wives liked to go shopping while their husbands gambled, and that there was a lot to be said for giving winners a chance to spend their gains before leaving town. Upscale shopping centers and designer outlets quickly appeared up and down the Strip, and today Las Vegas remains one of the West's most amazing shopping areas.

Las Vegas faced its greatest challenge in the 1990s, as gambling proliferated in the United States in the shape of Indian casinos, offshore casinos, and government lotteries.

No longer could gaming and a "sin city" reputation alone be relied on to sustain what had become one of the world's top tourist destinations. Las Vegas responded by transforming itself into a family entertainment mecca filled with theme-park attractions and extravagant architecture. The slot machines clang and the betting chips clatter as usual, but now they're just another phenomenon competing for your attention with 10-story Coca-Cola bottles, rooftop roller-coasters, albino tigers, simulated volcanos, and myriad other artificial wonders.

Suggested Schedule

Today   Arrive in Las Vegas by plane, car, or motor-home.

Tonight   Explore the sights of the city that never sleeps.

Tomorrow While playing tonight, keep in mind that tomorrow's schedule calls for up to 305 miles of driving, so you may want to get an early start. Or you may want to plan an extra day in Las Vegas first.

Orientation

Las Vegas's McCarran International Airport is located at the south end of the Strip, but the entrance is off Paradise Parkway. From Paradise, turn west on Tropicana or Flamingo Avenue and you'll run into the Strip, officially known as Las Vegas Boulevard South. You can't miss it: It's one of the most congested streets in the United States. Most hotels and sightseeing highlights covered in this chapter are along the Strip.

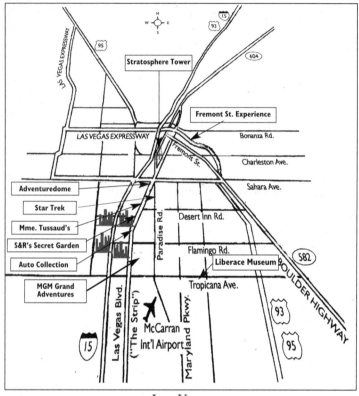

Las Vegas

If you're arriving by private vehicle, take Interstate 15 (which runs between Los Angeles and Salt Lake City) into town, get off at the Tropicana or Flamingo exit, and drive a short distance east to the Strip.

Whether you're driving your own vehicle or a rental, it's best to park it at your hotel and leave it there until you're ready to leave town. Many hotels have free shuttles that run up and down the Strip, and you can get anyplace on the Strip or downtown by public buses, which cost $2 (exact change) and run frequently.

Hotel Sightseeing Highlights

Stratosphere Tower—The Stratosphere Hotel claims this is the world's largest free-standing tower. True or not, it's the tallest structure in Las Vegas. From the observation deck at the top, you get an overview of the whole city and its surroundings from Mount Charleston to Lake Mead. Go at sunset and watch the lights of the Strip come on. Located at the Stratosphere Hotel, 2000 Las Vegas Boulevard South, (702) 382-7777, the tower's observation deck is open from 10:00 a.m. to 1:00 a.m. weekdays, until 2:00 a.m. Friday and Saturday. Admission $6 for adults, $3 for seniors and children ages 4 to 12.

Bellagio Impressionist Art Gallery—This multimillion-dollar art collection features works by Monet, Cezanne, Gauguin, and other French Impressionists of the period that inspired this elegant theme hotel's design. 3600 Las Vegas Boulevard South, (702) 693-7111. Admission is $10 per person. (By the way, if art is your passion, you can find works by Marc Chagall and Salvador Dali at the Las Vegas Art Museum, 900 Las Vegas Boulevard North, (702) 360-8080; open Tuesday through Saturday from 10:00 a.m. to 5:00 p.m., Sunday 1:00 to 5:00 p.m., admission $3 for adults, $1 for students and seniors.

MGM Grand Adventures—Amusement parks seem to be multiplying like jackrabbits in Las Vegas today, and kids I've consulted say this one is still the best. There are water park features, a roller-coaster and other carnival rides, a spectacular 250-foot-tall skydiving tower, theater shows and (as if you don't get enough re-creations of distant places just walking along the Strip) "villages" representing New Orleans, Salem, Asia, and other ports of call.

3799 Las Vegas Boulevard South, (702) 891-7979; open during daylight hours, times vary, $12.50 for nonguests, $10 for guests, free for kids under 3 feet 6 inches tall.

Adventuredome (Circus Circus)—Here's another theme park. Its distinction is that it's indoors, where it's cool on hot days. Featured are virtual reality games, water rides, and a roller-coaster that careens through a Jurassic landscape complete with life-size model dinosaurs. Adventuredome stays open until midnight daily in summer and on weekends the rest of the year. 2880 Las Vegas Boulevard South, (702) 794-3745; all-day pass $16.95 for adults, $12.95 for kids under 3 feet 6 inches tall.

Imperial Palace Antique and Classic Auto Collection— One of the finest vintage car collections anywhere features Adolf Hitler's Mercedes, John F. Kennedy's Lincoln, and Cadillacs that once belonged to Elvis Presley and Al Capone. 3535 Las Vegas Boulevard South, (702) 731-3311; open daily from 9:30 a.m. to 11:00 p.m., $6.95 for adults, $3 for seniors and children ages 5 to 11.

The Secret Garden of Siegfried and Roy (Mirage)— This outdoor habitat is where the magicians' collection of tigers and white lions prowl when not on stage. There is also a saltwater tank where frolicking bottlenose dolphins can be viewed from above or below water level. 3400 Las Vegas Boulevard South, (702) 791-7111; open weekdays except Wednesday from 11:00 a.m. to 5:00 p.m., weekends from 11:00 a.m. to 5:00 p.m., admission $10 for adults, accompanied children under 11 free.

Star Trek: The Experience (Las Vegas Hilton)— Trekkie heaven. Wait in a museum filled with *Star Trek* memorabilia, then board the starship *Enterprise* for a wild warp-speed ride and a battle with Klingons. The tilting-seat simulation is realistic enough that small children are not allowed. Located near the convention center at 3000 Paradise Road, (702) 697-8700; open daily from 11:00 a.m. to 11:00 p.m., $15.95 per person.

Free Spectacles—Don't miss the astonishing free attractions that hotels display along the Strip, such as: The **Battle of Buccaneer Bay** between British sailors and Spanish pirates from the decks of old-fashioned sailing ships every 90 minutes from 4:00 to 10:00 p.m. at Treasure Island (3300 Las Vegas Boulevard South); the 50-foot-tall **volcano** that blows its top every 15 minutes from sunset to midnight in front of the Mirage (3400 Las Vegas Boulevard South); the **Lago de Bellagio Fountains,** which shoot streams of water 240 feet in the air in a fantastic sound-and-light show every 15 minutes from 6:00 p.m. to midnight outside the Bellagio (3600 Las Vegas Boulevard South); the **fire-breathing dragon** that does battle with knights in armor and is slain and resurrected every hour on the hour from sunset to midnight in front of the Excalibur (3850 Las Vegas Boulevard South).

Other Sightseeing Highlights

Fremont Street Experience—Las Vegas has another casino-hotel district, the downtown area along Fremont Street traditionally known as "Glitter Gulch." Searching for a way to compete with the new theme-park atmosphere of the Strip, downtown hotels chipped in to create the Fremont Street Experience. A slatted roof was erected over 10 blocks of the street. It provides shade on hot days and after dark becomes one of the world's largest projection screens as sound-and-light shows are projected overhead. The free shows are offered every hour from dark until midnight, last about 20 minutes, and each one is different—you may see whales swimming overhead or witness a battle against alien spacecraft. Follow Las Vegas Boulevard north past the end of the Strip and it will take you directly downtown to Fremont Street.

Liberace Museum—The king of glam long before Elton John started piano lessons, Lee Liberace was the 1950s' most ostentatious entertainer. Three decades after his death, the museum exhibiting his furs, historic pianos, one-of-a-kind automobiles, and diamonds, diamonds, diamonds continues to be Las Vegas's most popular off-Strip attraction. 1775 East Tropicana Avenue, (702) 798-5595; open Monday through Saturday from 10:00 a.m. to 5:00 p.m., Sunday from 1:00 to 5:00 p.m., $6.95 for adults, $4.95 for seniors, 50¢ for students, free under 12.

Madame Tussaud's Celebrity Encounter—The best of several commercial attractions along the Strip, this wax museum puts you in a cocktail party setting with familiar faces in sports, politics, the movies, and music. A separate exhibit shows how Madame Tussaud's incredibly lifelike figures are made. Located at 3377 Las Vegas Boulevard South, (702) 367-1847; open daily from 10:00 a.m. to 11:00 p.m., $12.50 for adults, $10.75 for seniors, $10 for children ages 4 to 12.

Lodging

Regardless of budget, there's a lot to be said for picking a hotel with a reasonably central Strip location. Room rates are almost always lowest on Monday through Wednesday nights and highest on Friday and Saturday nights and whenever there's a large convention in town. Rates at the larger hotels are set by computer based on demand, so if you call today and then again tomorrow, you may get a different price. Advance reservations are essential, since Las Vegas hotels operate near capacity much of the time.

The new trend in Las Vegas Strip resorts is the theme hotel. True, there were hotels 20 or 30 years ago that adopted exotic motifs—Caesars Palace and the old Aladdin come to mind—but nothing like **Paris Las Vegas**, $95 to $300, 3655 Las Vegas Boulevard South, (702) 945-7000, the largest hotel in Las Vegas—and probably the world—with nearly 4000 guest rooms and grand-scale re-creations of the Eiffel Tower, Arc de Triomphe, Champs Elysées, Louvre, and River Seine; the **Venetian**, $130 to $700, 3355 Las Vegas Boulevard South, (702) 733-5000 or (888) 283-6423, an all-suite hotel with gondolas that travel along canals past re-creations of St. Mark's Square and the Doge's Palace; or **New York New York**, $80 and up, 3790 Las Vegas Boulevard South, (702) 740-6969 or 800-693-6763, where the guest-room towers are disguised as Big Apple skyscrapers, the casino is designed to be reminiscent of Central Park, a Coney Island roller-coaster careens around the hotel rooftops, and shop and restaurant facades recall New York neighborhoods from Greenwich Village to Wall Street; or the **Luxor**, $70 to $400, 3900 Las Vegas Boulevard South, (702) 262-4000. Top of the line in Las Vegas today, the **Bellagio**, $160 to $700, 3600 Las Vegas Boulevard South, (702) 693-7111 recreates the opulence of the dawn of the 20th century in a palace gleaming with polished marble.

Travelers on more limited budgets can find reasonably priced rooms at many of the older Strip hotels, among them **Circus Circus,** $60 and up, 2880 Las Vegas Boulevard South, (702) 734-0410, and the **Imperial Palace,** $55 and up, 3535 Las Vegas Boulevard South, (702) 731-3311, which has a central location and walk-out balconies—a rarity in a city where most hotel room windows won't open because of concerns about suicide. The newly renovated **Caesars Palace**, $90 and up, 3570 Las Vegas Boulevard South, (702) 731-7110, once considered the ultimate Las Vegas luxury hotel, offers a bargain on oversized, well-appointed rooms.

For homelike budget lodgings just off the Strip, check out the **Somerset House Motel,** $35 to $44, 294 Convention Center Drive, (702) 735-4411. Guest rooms in this former apartment house vary widely in space and furnishings, though the rates are about the same for all.

Food

All-you-can-eat buffets have been features of virtually all Las Vegas casino hotels since the 1950s, when they were the quick, cheap place to eat, leaving more in your pocket to gamble away when you leave. Today's buffets have evolved, offering international and even gourmet cuisine at prices in the $15 to $20 range for dinner. There's no need for reservations, and you can sample a wide variety of dishes or suit your meal to vegetarian or other food preferences. To avoid long lines, go at off-hours—breakfast at 7:00 or 10:00, lunch at 11:00 or 2:00, dinner at 4:00 or 9:00.

Top of the line is the **Bellagio Buffet,** 3600 Las Vegas Boulevard South, (702) 693-7111, where you can feast on fresh seafood, smoked sturgeon, marinated steaks, and muscovy duck for $15 lunch or $20 dinner. Their top competition is **Le Village Buffet** in Paris Las Vegas, 3655 Las Vegas Boulevard South; (702) 945-7000, featuring seafood quiche, venison stew, green-lip mussels in tarragon cream sauce—all that French stuff—for $11 lunch or $22 dinner. For exotic and eclectic fare, it's hard to beat the **Spice Market Buffet** in the Aladdin Hotel, 3667 Las Vegas Boulevard South, (702) 785-5555, with its lavish spread of Middle Eastern dishes alongside assortments of Mexican, Asian, Italian and seafood favorites, all for $13 lunch, $19 dinner or $16 Sunday champagne brunch. If you're nostalgic for the days when Vegas buffets served regular food, you'll find all-you-can-eat of it at the **Stratosphere Buffet,** 2000 Las Vegas Boulevard South, (702) 382-7777, for just $6.50 lunch or $8 dinner.

Besides buffets, all casino hotels on the Strip feature a selection of full-service restaurants in all price ranges. Many have 20 or more places to eat, from quick coffee shops to purveyors of haute cuisine at high-roller prices. Standouts include designer restaurant mogul Wolfgang Puck's two midpriced showplaces, the eclectically Asian **Chinois,** (702) 737-9700, and the California-Italian **Spago,** (702) 369-6300, both in the Forum shopping area at Caesars Palace, 3570 Las Vegas Boulevard South. Call ahead for reservations. For *nouveau* pizzas with Thai chicken, Caribbean shrimp, or barbecue toppings, check out the **California Pizza Kitchen** in the Mirage, 3400 Las Vegas Boulevard South, (702) 791-7357, with a second location downtown in the Golden Nugget, 129 East Fremont Street, (702) 385-7111.

Las Vegas also has more than its share of good restaurants that are not in casinos. Most of them aim for a mainly local clientele. Many specialize in international and exotic cuisines and are more affordable than their casino counterparts. A few suggestions that are easy to find from the Strip: the Ethiopean **Horn of Africa** at 1510 South Las Vegas Boulevard, (702) 383-6741; the Cuban **Florida Café**, 1401 Las Vegas Boulevard South, (702) 385-3013; the buffet-style **India Palace**, 505 East Twain Avenue, (702) 796-4177; the **Mediterranean Café and Market** and adjoining **Hookah Lounge**, both at 4147 South Maryland Parkway, (702) 731-6030; and the vegetarian **Rainbow's End**, 1100 East Sahara Avenue, (702) 737-7282. Or, if you're wondering what ever happened to good old American road food, find out at the **Harley Davidson Café**, 3725 Las Vegas Boulevard South, (702) 740-4555.

Camping

Circusland, the 420-site RV campground operated by Circus Circus behind the hotel, (702) 734-0410, bills itself as "The World's Finest RV Park." Well . . . the scenery may leave something to be desired, but it is within convenient walking distance of the "World's Largest Curio Shop." Amenities include a pool, Jacuzzi, children's playground, laundry and 24-hour convenience store, and full hookups. An elevated tramway carries campers to the hotel's casino.

Valley of Fire State Park Campground (see Day 2) has 38 campsites, picnic tables, and running water. Staying here enables you to explore the park early in the morning when it's cool and the sand is covered with animal tracks.

South along Lake Mead Drive, you'll find lakeside camping at Overton Beach, Echo Bay, and Hemenway Beach.

Nightlife

Las Vegas showrooms have been legendary since the 1950s. Today fewer hotels present limited-run shows by famous-name entertainers. There are many more big-budget productions packed with special effects and scheduled to run indefinitely. Most big-name shows cost $60 to $90 a person; impersonation and nostalgia shows run $25 to $30. Order your tickets early, as famous-name concerts sell out as much as two months in advance.

Among the top continuous-run shows, the Tropicana's **Folies Bergere,** 3801 Las Vegas Boulevard South, (702) 739-2222, has been around the longest--more than 40 years. Also an everlasting favorite, **Siegfried & Roy**'s blend of magic and animal training at the Mirage, 3400 Las Vegas Boulevard South, (702) 791-7111, is probably the priciest showroom act on the Strip at $100.50 a ticket. New York New York, 3790 Las Vegas Boulevard South, (702) 740-6969, presents **Lord of the Dance,** the Irish stepdancing production direct from its Broadway run. The French-Canadian–Chinese circus and dance troop **Cirque du Soliel,** which has staged shows at various Las Vegas venues over the years, is now performing a new show simply called **O** at the Bellagio, 3600 Las Vegas Boulevard South, (702) 693-7111. Perhaps the most bizarre show on the Strip is the long-running **An Evening at La Cage,** a partly improv lineup of female impersonators, at the Riviera, 2901 Las Vegas Boulevard South, (702) 734-5110. No, Wait . . . even La Cage can't offer the surreal experience that the Luxor's **Blue Man Group,** 3900 Las Vegas Boulevard South, (702) 262-4000, does with its amazing mix of mime, acrobatics, homemade instruments, and noise.

In fact, impersonation is a big business in Las Vegas clubs. You'll find Elvis impersonator shows at several places. The best of the bunch, **American Superstar** at the Stratosphere, 2000 Las Vegas Boulevard, (702) 382-7777, features not only a great artificial Elvis but also impersonations of Charlie Daniels, Madonna, Michael Jackson, and Gloria Estefan.

You'll also find plenty of genuine old-timers on the concert schedules. Nostalgia is king at the **Suncoast**, 9090 Alta Drive, (702) 636-7111, where recent entertainers have included the Kingston Trio, Al Martino, and the Lettermen. The **Orleans**, 4500 West Tropicana Boulevard, (702) 365-7111, also presents entertainers from your youth (or maybe your parents'); recent acts have included Peter, Paul & Mary, the Smothers Brothers, Neil Sedaka, and Frankie Avalon and Bobby Rydell on a double bill. The calendar of the **Las Vegas Hilton,** 3000 Paradise Road, (702) 732-5111, features an eclectic array of singers from yesteryear, including recently the Four Tops, Smokey Robinson, Olivia Newton-John, Alabama, and Toto. But for the ultimate in Las Vegas nostalgia, check out the **Wayne Newton Theatre** in the Stardust, 3000 Las Vegas Boulevard South, (800) 824-6033; besides Newton, one of the most popular performers in Las Vegas history, the theater hosts other Vegas legends like Don Rickles.

Prefer something a little more contemporary? Try the **Paris Las Vegas**, 3655 Las Vegas Boulevard South, (702) 946-7000, which presents concerts by a full range of performers from Earth, Wind & Fire to Natalie Cole, and from Julio Iglesias to Clint Black. The best concert venue in town, though, is not a hotel but the **House of Blues**, 3950 Las Vegas Boulevard South, (702) 632-7600, where recent artists have ranged from Etta James to KC and the Sunshine Band.

Comedy is in the spotlight at several hotels, and if you check the current schedule you're likely to find not only the top new comics but also Vegas veterans like Howie Mandel, David Brenner, Tim Conway, Harvey Korman, and the Second City Improv Company. The MGM Grand's **Hollywood Theatre**, 3799 Las Vegas Boulevard South, (702) 891-1111, alternates famous-name comics as diverse as Rodney Dangerfield, George Carlin, and Carrot Top with perennial singers like Paul Anka and Tom Jones. The hotel also introduces new comedy acts at its "Catch a Rising Star" lounge show.

Bookstores

Not long ago there wasn't a bookstore in Las Vegas; hoteliers didn't want guests to waste time reading when they could be in the casinos losing money. That has changed, though. Today, besides major-chain bookstores, Las Vegas supports nearly 70 independent booksellers. The majority of them specialize in adult erotica, Mormon religious books, or new age and metaphysical books. Here are some of Las Vegas's leading general-interest indies.

The Book Shoppe, 2232 South Nellis Boulevard, (702) 641-1155.

Dead Poet Bookstore, 3874 West Sahara Avenue, (702) 227-4070.

Genesis Books, 1815 West Charleston Boulevard, (702) 386-0099.

Get Booked, 4640 Paradise Road, (702) 737-7780.

Great Wall Bookstore, 4255 Spring Mountain Road, (702) 876-8875.

Lake Mead to London Bridge

Today's picturesque desert drive takes you through the fantastic white and red sandstone formations of the Valley of Fire, then along the Lake Mead shore before visiting Hoover Dam, the oldest dam on the Colorado River—and the most crowded. It's such a big tourist draw that it needs a multilevel parking lot.

After the Colorado River spills through the huge generators at Hoover Dam, it continues into a series of other dams and reservoirs. None of these desert lakes is anywhere near the size of Lake Powell or Lake Mead. In most places, they still look like a river—but a deep, lazy river as wide as the Mississippi, nothing like the whitewater torrent that crashes through the Grand Canyon a hundred or so miles upriver. Hoover Dam tamed the river. The other dams and resort towns downstream use it. As much as one-third of the water in the Colorado River evaporates from the surface of the manmade lakes as it makes its way through the harsh, sun-baked Mohave Desert. The rest is diverted to irrigate farmland in southern California. By the time the river reaches the Mexican border and the delta where it used to flow into the Sea of Cortés, there is no water left in it.

We're not going that far today, though. Heading south through the Mojave Desert brings you to the riverside casino town of Laughlin, where you'll cross the Colorado River into Arizona. Continuing downriver, you'll come to one of the most improbable sights anywhere—the old London Bridge, moved stone-by-stone to be reconstructed over an artificial canal in the desert.

Return to Laughlin to spend the night, or follow old Route 66 through the ghost town of Oatman and spend the night in Kingman.

Suggested Schedule

9:00 a.m.	Leave Las Vegas. Explore the Valley of Fire and Lake Mead Scenic Drive.
12:30 p.m.	Cross Davis Dam into Arizona at Laughlin/Bullhead City.
2:00 p.m.	Arrive in Lake Havasu City. Late lunch by London Bridge.
3:30 p.m.	Visit Oatman.
4:30 p.m.	Drive to Kingman or Laughlin.
5:00 p.m.	Check into your accommodations at Kingman or Laughlin, or camp at Hualapai Mountain Park.

Travel Route: Las Vegas to Laughlin (305 miles)

Leaving Las Vegas, drive 33 miles northbound on Interstate 15, take the Glendale exit and follow NV 169 south to Overton, where you may wish to visit the Lost City Museum (721 South Moapa Valley Road, 702-397-2193, open daily from 8:30 a.m. to 4:30 p.m.; $2 for adults, free for children and students under 18), a com-

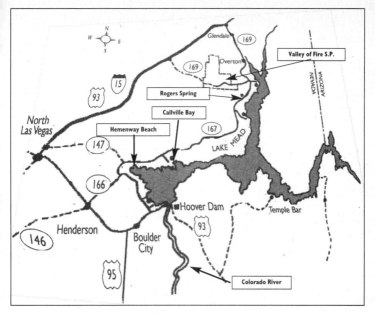

Lake Mead Area

prehensive exhibit about the early Pueblo people who thrived here around A.D. 800. Past Overton, take the well-marked road that turns right (west) to Valley of Fire State Park.

After exploring the Valley of Fire, where the park road intersects the Lake Mead Scenic Drive, turn left (or continue straight for a brief stop at Overton Beach, 2 miles farther on, then return to the Lake Mead road).

A few miles south of the beach, the road joins US 93. Turn left (east) and descend by switchbacks to Hoover Dam. Leaving Hoover Dam, stay on US 93 through Boulder City, which was the largest town in southern Nevada before World War II. Turn south on US 95, where the sign says "Searchlight/Needles." Go 54 miles south on this highway, through the stark rocky hills and dry lake beds of the Mohave Desert, and turn left (east) on NV 163. It's 21 miles to Davis Dam, which contains Lake Mohave, the next Colorado River reservoir south of Lake Mead. The casino strip of Laughlin is 3 miles below the dam on the Nevada side.

Cross the dam into Arizona. Because Arizona does not believe in Daylight Savings Time, you change time zones here in the winter but not in the summer. As you cross the dam, NV 163 becomes AZ 68. Turn south on AZ 95 (State Highway 95, which follows the east bank of the Colorado River, not US 95 on the Nevada/California side of the river). Bullhead City is 3 miles south of Davis Dam on the Arizona side.

Continue south on AZ 95 for 39 miles to Topock, where it joins Interstate 40. Take the interstate east for two exits (about 9 miles) and exit south on AZ 95. It is 21 miles from the interstate to Lake Havasu City.

Upon leaving Lake Havasu City, retrace your route north to I 40 and Topock. Take AZ 95 for 4 miles north from Topock. Where the road forks near Golden Shores Marina, take a right. From there, the narrow, crumbling paved road that, incredibly, was once part of Route 66, the main highway to southern California, goes about 20 miles to Oatman, then another 27 miles over the crest of a small mountain range to return to I 40 at Kingman.

If you plan to stay in Laughlin tonight, the more direct way to get back there from Kingman is to take AZ 68 due west for 28 miles to the river, a spectacular trip through a lunar landscape.

Sightseeing Highlights

Valley of Fire State Park—White and red sandstone layers have fractured and eroded into a bewildering maze, best appreciated on a short hike into Mouse's Tank, where an Indian renegade named Old Mouse and about 50 followers hid out while raiding area ranches. It took the cavalry 11 years to find them. Thousand-year-old petroglyphs, scratched with wooden *atlatls* (spear-throwing sticks) in the soft stone surfaces by nomadic Indian hunters, decorate the walls of several canyons within the park. Hiking is best soon after dawn, when tracks of nighttime wildlife are fresh and the large white nocturnal flowers of the sacred datura are still open. You might even catch a rare glimpse of a desert bighorn sheep. Park admission is $5 per vehicle. Open daily from 8:30 a.m. to 4:00 p.m. (702) 397-2088.

Lake Mead Scenic Drive—The Lake Mead Scenic Drive parallels the shoreline for 42 miles, but for the first hour of the drive you won't see the lake from the road; instead, you'll follow dry Las Vegas Wash. Stop and let tiny tropical fish nibble your toes in Rogers Warm Spring, on your right. For a lake view, visit Echo Bay, 2 miles down a road on your left. You know you're nearing the end of the Lake Mead road when you see often-lively Hemenway Beach and its campground. Stop and splash. The water's fine, though you'll want sandals because the beach is rocky. Warm and cold convection currents in the lake water tingle swimmers' skin. Use caution when wading: this is the rim of a flooded canyon, and not far from shore, submerged cliffs drop off into water 400 feet deep. (702) 293-6180.

Hoover Dam—The oldest dam on the Colorado River, completed in 1935, Hoover Dam has become a major tourist attraction with the growth of Las Vegas. You can walk on top of the dam for free. Check out the dam's unusual art deco ornamentation, including winged sculptures called Figures of the Republic and a terrazzo representation of the solar system with astrological overtones. Visitors are prohibited from carrying bags, including purses, daypacks, and large camera cases, onto the dam because of government concerns about terrorism.

Tours cost $8 for adults, $7 for seniors, $2 for students ages 6 to 16; a longer "hardhat tour" costs $25 per person, and reservations are recommended. They take you by elevator down through the center of the dam to the power plant, daily from 8:00 a.m. to 6:45 p.m. Memorial Day to Labor Day, 9:00 a.m. to 4:15 p.m. the rest of the year. See the large relief map of the Colorado River in the visitors center, which is open daily from 8:00 a.m. to 5:45 p.m. and charges $4 admission for adults, $2 for students ages 6 to 16. (702) 293-8990.

Bullhead City and Laughlin—With a population of more than 25,000, Bullhead City is the fastest-growing city in Arizona. It has warm weather in winter and a great location for fishing and boating on the river between Lake Mohave and Lake Havasu. The community's only industry is casino hotels, located on the Nevada side of the river in Laughlin, a town without much in the way of residential or commercial areas. The casinos, hotels, and restaurants of Laughlin provide most of the employment not only for Bullhead City but also for residents of Kingman, Arizona, and Needles, California.

Laughlin casinos make most of their money on week-

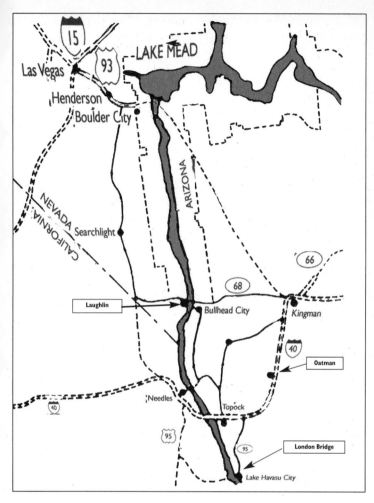

Las Vegas to London Bridge

ends, when people arrive from Phoenix, just four hours away. On weekdays, this fast-growing casino row caters primarily to motor home travelers, for whom the miles and miles of free RV parking lots (no facilities) make

Laughlin much easier than Las Vegas. Coming from Las Vegas, you'll find Laughlin anticlimactic, though the whole casino row fronts on the Colorado River with a beachfront that any Las Vegas hotel might envy. Oldtimers say Laughlin reminds them of Las Vegas in the 1950s.

Lake Havasu State Park—Almost all of the Arizona shore of Lake Havasu is a state park, with campgrounds, boat ramps, and small swimming beaches at Windsor Beach and Crystal Beach, right in Lake Havasu City, as well as at Cattail Cove, 15 miles south of town. The scenic Mohave Sunset Trail runs for 2 miles between Windsor Beach and Crystal Beach, over rocky desert ridgelines and through dense riverside stands of tamarisk. Fifteen miles south of town, there are more camping, boating, and water sports facilities at Cattail Cove. Besides these areas, the park takes in the Aubrey Hills Natural Area, a wild shoreline that can't be reached by road.

London Bridge—Lake Havasu City (pop. 25,000) is "the most successful free-standing new town in the United States," according to the *Los Angeles Times*. It was founded less than 30 years ago by two partners, chainsaw king Robert McCulloch and developer C. V. Wood Jr., who had recently retired from his position as general manager of Disneyland. Carefully planning each smallest detail of their dream community, they decided that they needed a tourist attraction to lure visitors off the interstate and prime the local economy. So they bought the London Bridge, which was being replaced and auctioned off by the city of London.

The bridge, built in 1825 to replace a still older London Bridge, is the same one Charles Dickens and Sir Arthur Conan Doyle wrote about. After buying it for $2,460,000,

McCulloch and Wood disassembled it into stone blocks weighing from 1,000 to 17,000 pounds each, then transported the 10,000 tons of granite for 10,000 miles to reassemble it on the shore of Lake Havasu. Finally, they dredged a canal to let water flow under the bridge. Most onlookers scoffed at the time, seeing the London Bridge project as the all-time greatest folly ever perpetrated by a land developer. But it worked. Today, the London Bridge is the second-most-popular tourist attraction in Arizona, surpassed only by the Grand Canyon. You can drive across the bridge or walk across. It's open 24 hours a day, and it's free.

Oatman—Some towns just won't die. The gold boomtown of Oatman thrived from 1906 to 1942, when the mines closed. It could easily have dried up and blown away like its sister community, Goldroad, a few miles up the highway, where buildings were pulled apart for firewood and demolished to the foundations to reduce property taxes. But Oatman's buildings were saved thanks to motion picture companies who preserved it as a location for cowboy movies. Today, tourism keeps Oatman going. Wild burros, descendants of animals that worked in the mines, wander the streets of town panhandling for snacks. Oatman gets lively on weekends with bluegrass music and mock shootouts in the streets. The most interesting sight in town is the funky "honeymoon suite" in the old Oatman Hotel, where Clark Gable and Carole Lombard spent their wedding night en route back to Hollywood after their surprise marriage ceremony in Kingman.

Mohave Museum of History and Arts—Kingman, Arizona, is the world's leading producer of jewelry-grade turquoise, and this museum features the Colbaugh

Collection of carved turquoise, some local and more from places as distant as Persia. The museum also has displays of regional history from prehistoric times to the present, a miniature Mohave Indian village diorama, and a room memorializing Kingman's most famous native son, the late actor Andy ("Hey, Wild Bill, wait for me!") Devine. Located a quarter-mile east of the Beale Street exit from I 40, the museum is open Monday through Friday from 9:00 a.m. to 5:00 p.m., Saturday and Sunday 1:00 to 5:00 p.m. Admission is $3 for adults, 50 cents for children under 12.

Hualapai Mountain Park—When was the last time you saw a pine tree? You'll find cool mountain forests and great scenic views just 14 miles southeast of Kingman on paved Hualapai Mountain Road. This 2,200-acre county park, set at 5,000 feet elevation with mountain peaks rising to 8,000 feet, has picnic grounds and more than ten miles of hiking trails. Abundant wildlife includes deer, elk, and coyotes, as well as many species of birds not often seen in the Mohave Desert. (928) 757-0915.

Food and Lodging

For low-cost luxury lodging, your best bet is to spend the night in Laughlin. On Sunday through Thursday nights, spacious, nicely furnished modern rooms at almost any of the ten big casino hotels cost less than accommodations in the standard roadside motels in Kingman—or just about anyplace else in the Southwest. Laughlin room rates often more than double on weekends. The largest hotel in Laughlin is also the oldest, dating back to 1977, when Don Laughlin bought the Riverside Bait Shop, incorporated its site as a town, and expanded it into the 661-room **Riverside Resort,** (702) 298-2535. Rooms start at $25 on weeknights, much higher on weekends. At the **Colorado Belle,** (702) 298-4000, a showy hotel built in the shape of a giant riverboat by the same company as Circus Circus and Excalibur in Las Vegas, rates start at $25 on weeknights. Similar rates are available at the **Edgewater,** (702) 298-2453, and the **Flamingo Laughlin,** (702) 298-5111. The finest hotel in town, over the crest of a ridge from the rest of casino row, is the Mexican-theme **Harrah's,** (702) 298-4600, where rates range from $35 to $55 on weeknights. All of these hotels have swimming pools, spas, beaches on the river, and of course gambling casinos. They also have good, inexpensive all-you-can-eat buffets as well as coffee shops and full-service restaurants.

The most interesting accommodations in the Kingman area are at the **Hualapai Mountain Lodge,** (928) 757-3435. The rustic lodge, built at Hualapai Mountain Park by the Civilian Conservation Corps in the 1930s, rents cabins for about $55 a night. There is a restaurant and a grocery store on the premises.

Camping

Hualapai Mountain Park outside of Kingman has 67 tent campsites and 11 RV sites with hookups. There are drinking water and rest rooms—no showers. The setting, in a shady island of mountain forest above the sunbaked Mohave Desert, is wonderful for evening and early morning walks.

You can camp free at Wild Cow Campground, six miles

past the county park on Hualapai Mountain Road. There are pit toilets but no drinking water or hook-ups at this 20-site campground operated by the Bureau of Land Management. Open from May through October only.

Hiking and Boating

Hualapai Mountain Park has a six-mile network of trails up, over and around the mountain's cool pine and aspen forests.

Boat rentals are available in Lake Havasu City. Contact Island Boat Rentals, 1580 Dover Avenue, (928) 453-3260; Lake Havasu Marina, 1100 McCullock Boulevard, (928) 855-2159; or Resort Boat Rentals, English Village, (928) 453-9613. Many excursion boats also cruise the lake from London Bridge. Canoes are for rent in Topock at the Jerkwater Canoe Company (928) 768-7753, to explore the Havasu-Topock National Wildlife Refuge at the north end of the lake.

Nightlife

If your travel style includes wine, music, and song, Laughlin is your best bet on the lower Colorado River. All of the casinos have free lounges with live entertainment nightly. The Riverside Resort is the only place in town with a Las Vegas–style dinner showroom. They feature big-name acts like the Gatlin Brothers, the Oak Ridge Boys, and Willie Nelson. Sam's Town Gold River offers Sandy Hackett's Comedy Club, where stand-up comics do dinner shows and late shows Wednesday through Saturday nights.

Bookstores

A preponderance of the independent bookstores in the Colorado River region are used paperback exchanges; some also sell new books of regional appeal. Among them are:

Mary's Book Exchange, 1570 Northern Avenue, Kingman, (928) 757-9495.

The Book Exchange, 1761 McCullock Boulevard North, Lake Havasu City, (928) 453-4043.

You'll find a good selection of regional titles at Hastings Books, Music & Video, 1985 Highway 95, Bullhead City, (928) 763-0025.

Route 66 and Sedona

Through western Arizona, old Route 66 followed a different route than today's Interstate 40 does. You drove part of that route through Oatman yesterday. This morning you can travel the rest of it (or skip it and take the interstate). In the afternoon, visit two historic old towns—Prescott, the first territorial capital, and Jerome, a once-rich mining town—to end the day in the contemporary resort community of Sedona. This route offers recreation and sightseeing choices that range from Indian ruins and exceptional historical museums to hiking trails and lakes. It's one of the most varied scenic drives in Arizona.

Suggested Schedule

8:30 a.m.	Breakfast
9:30 a.m.	Drive old Route 66 to Ash Fork
11:30 a.m.	Lunch in Prescott. Visit Sharlot Hall Museum.
12:30 p.m.	Drive over the mountains to Jerome.
2:00 p.m.	Stroll the old-time streets of Jerome.
3:00 p.m.	Drive to Tuzigoot National Monument.

4:00 p.m.   Drive to Sedona.

5:00 p.m.   Check into your lodging in Sedona or Oak Creek Canyon.

Travel Route: Kingman via Prescott to Sedona (234 miles)

To take the scenic, historic, but slower route, stay on AZ 66 as it parallels the railroad tracks northeast from Kingman. This alternate route is a segment of the original Route 66 that was abandoned by the federal government when the interstate was opened. It's 93 miles on a 55-mph two-lane highway to reach Seligman, which is 73 miles down the interstate from Kingman. Old Route 66 takes you among gentle hills on a historic road where not many vehicles travel these days.

The only sightseeing attraction along this stretch of old Route 66 is Grand Canyon Caverns, a large limestone cave 200 feet underground. Open from 8:00 a.m. to 6:00 p.m. in the summer months and 9:00 a.m. to 5:00 p.m. the rest of the year, the 45-minute cave tour is $8.50 for adults, $5.75 for children ages 6 to 14. As at so many tourist caves, there's a huge dinosaur statue by the entrance. Near the caverns is the turnoff to Supai (see the Itinerary Option at the end of this chapter). Near the turnoff you'll pass Peach Springs, the 800-person village that serves as the capital of the 1,000,000-acre Hualapai Reservation.

Upon returning to Interstate 40 at Seligman, continue east for 25 miles to Ash Fork. Exit there on US 89 southbound and drive 52 miles to Prescott. About 6 miles north of Prescott on US 89, a different highway called US 89A turns east. It goes 58 miles, over the mountains and through Jerome to Sedona.

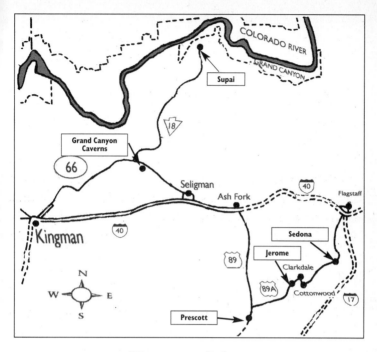

Kingman to Sedona

Sightseeing Highlights

Prescott—Tucked away between granite hills, Prescott is a lovely little town that seems to be left over from an earlier era. The first capital of the Arizona Territory, Prescott is one of the oldest towns in the state, dating back to the 1860s. As you stroll down the small-town main street, you may feel that you've been spirited back through time to the 1950s. The lawn of the grand old courthouse has shade trees and larger-than-life bronze statues of Old West life. Wholesome Norman Rockwell–style quaintness coexists with Whisky Row, a notorious block of Old West saloons that are still in operation after all these years.

Downtown Prescott is a good place to shop for antiques, too. Until you drive out of town and into suburban Prescott Valley, it's hard to believe that this is one of the fastest-growing communities in Arizona.

The major sightseeing attraction in Prescott is the **Sharlot Hall Museum**, 415 W. Gurley Street, (928) 445-3122. Perhaps Arizona's finest historical museum of the territorial era, this large park contains several 19th-century structures, most of which have been moved here from different parts of central Arizona, including two former governor's mansions. There are Victorian furnishings, ranch antiques, Indian artifacts, and a sizable collection of stagecoaches and other horse-drawn vehicles. The museum is named after its founder, Sharlot Hall. An explorer, essayist, and poet, she became the official historian of the Arizona Territory in 1909. Sharlot Hall Museum is open Monday through Saturday from 10:00 a.m. to 5:00 p.m. (closing at 4:00 p.m. November through March) and Sunday from 1:00 to 5:00 p.m. year-round. Donations are welcome.

Other highlights for those who choose to spend extra time exploring Prescott include the **Phippen Museum of Western Art**, 4701 US 89 North, (928) 778-1385, which displays works by more than 80 contemporary painters and sculptors (open Monday and Wednesday through Saturday from 10:00 a.m. to 4:00 p.m. and Sunday 1:00 to 4:00 p.m.; **The Bead Museum**, 140 S. Montezuma Street, on Whisky Row, exhibiting one of the world's largest collections of beads and explaining their many uses throughout history (open Monday through Saturday from 9:30 a.m. to 4:30 p.m., donations welcome); and the **Smoki Museum**, 100 N. Arizona Avenue, (928) 445-

1230, displaying a large collection of authentic and spurious Indian artifacts owned by the Smokis, a local "tribe" of "Wannabe Indians" that has been headquartered in Prescott for 70 years (open during the summer months only, Monday through Saturday from 10:00 a.m. to 4:00 p.m., Sunday 1:00 to 4:00 p.m., adults $4, seniors $3, students $2, under 12 free).

Jerome—High on a mountainside midway between Prescott and Sedona, Jerome was the site of environmental plunder on a grand scale. Paradoxically, it is now one of the most charming communities in central Arizona. Named after a cousin of Jennie Jerome (Winston Churchill's mother), the town had a population of 15,000 near the end of the 19th century, most of the residents living in tents. In 72 years, $800,000,000 worth of copper was dug from the mountainside, along with modest amounts of gold and silver. (Imagine 80 billion pennies. Stacked, they would make a column 63,000 miles tall. Laid in a row, they would reach almost a million miles. You could pave every inch of the U.S. interstate highway system with pennies and have more than a million dollars left over.)

Jerome was destroyed by fire three times in three years (1897-1899). One of the fires, a Prescott newspaper reported, wiped out the entire downtown area, consisting of 24 saloons, 14 Chinese restaurants, several casinos, and the red-light district. After the third fire, the town was rebuilt in brick. Jerome was abandoned in 1953 when the mines closed down.

Jerome is a National Historic District. Since the 1960s it has been repopulated, mainly by artists and craftspeople, to a present population of about 500. Visit the **Gold**

King Mine and Museum, the **Jerome Historical Society Mine Museum,** or the **Jerome State Historic Park Museum,** but the town's real charm is to be found all along the switchback main street with its folksy array of galleries, eateries, and rock shops.

Tuzigoot National Monument—Ruins of a white stone Sinagua Indian pueblo occupied in the 9th through 13th centuries stand atop a hill that now overlooks a slag field from the abandoned refinery that used to process the ore from Jerome's mines. The museum at the monument has a fine collection of artifacts found while excavating the site. Tuzigoot National Monument is located off the main highway 2 miles east of Clarkdale, (928) 634-5564. It is open daily in the summer months from 8:00 a.m. to 7:00 p.m., the rest of the year from 8:00 a.m. to 5:00 p.m. Admission is $2 per adult, children and students under 17 free.

Sedona—Perched between blistering desert lowlands and cool mountain forests in the heart of Arizona's Red Rock Country, this booming resort town has grown from a handful of pioneering residents to a year-round population of 12,000 in just 20 years. It has more millionaires per capita than any other municipality in the state, and it is the New Age capital of the known universe. Sedona has no museums or other conventional sightseeing highlights. The top activities are shopping and exploring the spectacular landscape that surrounds the town.

Shoppers will find dozens of galleries, boutiques, and cute little stores throughout uptown Sedona. The most enjoyable place to browse is the large, Spanish Colonial-style Tlaquepaque shop and restaurant complex on AZ 179 south of the "Y" (the junction of highways 179 and 89A).

More mysterious than Sedona's highly hyped "vortexes" are the traces left behind by the Sinagua people, who lived in the Sedona area in the 12th and 13th centuries—and by other ancient people who came before them. Easiest to reach is the V-Bar-V Ranch Petroglyph Site, where you'll find more than a thousand Sinagua rock art images of humans and animals. To get there, take I 17 east to exit 298 and follow the signs. Some of the largest Sinagua cliff dwellings in the area, along with cave paintings that date back long before the Sinaguas arrived, can be seen at Palatki Ruins and Honanki Cliff Dwellings, two sites the Forest Service recently opened to the public. To get there, take Highway 89A south of Sedona for 10 miles, then turn right on unpaved Forest Road 525. In a few miles you'll come to a well-marked fork where one road goes to Palatki and the other to Honanki. For information on all three sites, call (928) 282-4119.

Lodging

Most accommodations in the Sedona area are upscale. Among the best is **L'Auberge de Sedona**, 301 L'Auberge Lane, $210 to $430, (928) 282-7131, a French Provincial-style country inn in a secluded creekside location within walking distance of the center of town. Look for genuinely historic lodgings at **Bed and Breakfast at Saddle Rock Ranch**, 255 Rock Ridge Drive, $149 to $179, (928) 282-7640, a three-unit B-and-B in a stone and adobe ranch house that dates back to 1926. If room rates like these sound astronomical, compare them to the Sedona area's really high-end accommodations such as the huge **Enchantment Resort**, 525 Boynton Canyon Road, (928)

282-2900, where rooms start at $200 in the slow season and run $350 to $1050 in spring and fall.

In Oak Creek Canyon, lodgings range from the motel-style **Slide Rock Lodge**, $59 to $99, (928) 282-3531, to chic one- and two-bedroom condos with kitchens and fireplaces at **Junipine Resort**, $170 to $300, (928) 282-3375.

Relatively low-priced lodging can be found in Sedona at the **Matterhorn Lodge**, $59 to $119, 230 Apple Avenue, (928) 282-7176 or the **Sedona Motel**, $89 to $250, AZ 179 one block south of the "Y," (928) 282-7187. If budget is of primary concern, though, you'll get more for your money by pushing on and spending the night in Flagstaff (see tomorrow's listings).

Food

For lunch in Prescott, try **Murphy's**, a historic downtown restaurant at 201 North Cortez, (928) 445-4044, a restored 1890 store where moderately priced pasta, seafood, and beef entrées are served. Nearby, another local favorite in a historic building, the **Gurley Street Grill**, 230 West Gurley Street, (928) 445-3388, features pizzas, cheeseburgers, chicken, and other affordable fare. Or dine in Hassayampa Hotel's **Peacock Room**, 122 East Gurley Street, (928) 778-9434, with its steak-and-seafood menu and yesteryear elegance.

Stop for a pastry and a cup of gourmet coffee in Jerome at the **Flatiron Café**, 416 Main Street, (928) 634-2733, where the menu includes tempting vegetarian options. The view of the valley below is part of the appeal at the not-so-veggie **Jerome Palace Haunted Burger**, 401

Clark Street, (928) 634-0554, where you can also get bar-becued ribs or chicken.

In Sedona, you can enjoy one of the best (and priciest) Continental dinners in the Southwest at the country French style **L'Auberge de Sedona Restaurant**, 301 L'Auberge Lane, (928) 282-7131, where the fixed-price six-course bill of fare changes nightly (coat and tie required). Another excellent, expensive restaurant is **René at Tlaquepaque**, AZ 179 South, (928) 282-9225, serving traditional French cuisine in an Old Mexico atmosphere.

Heaping portions of standard Southwestern cuisine at affordable prices are the claims to fame at the **Javelina Cantina**, 671 Highway 179, (928) 282-1313, in the Hillside Marketplace. Or continue a few miles farther south to the Sedona suburb of Oak Creek, where the colorfully decorated **Wild Toucan Restaurant**, 6376 Highway 179, (928) 284-1608, features creative Mexican food. Look in the roadside shopping centers of West Sedona, along US 89A west of the "Y," for other affordable restaurants such as the **Lotus Garden**, 164 Coffee Pot Drive, (928) 282-3118, a Chinese restaurant in the Basha's Shopping Center.

Camping

The best camping spots around Sedona are at a series of campgrounds operated by the National Forest Service in Oak Creek Canyon. **Manzanita Campground**, 6 miles north of Sedona, has 19 sites. **Cave Spring Campground**, 12 miles north of town, has 78 sites, and **Pine Flat Campground**, a mile farther up the canyon, has 58. All are along the creek, and none has RV hookups. These campgrounds are only open from mid-May through mid-September, and they are crowded all summer. If no sites are available here, look for campgrounds in the Flagstaff area (see tomorrow's listings).

Hiking and Biking

An easy hike in the Prescott area is the 1.7-mile loop trail that goes from Thumb Butte Park on the edge of town up onto Thumb Butte for good views of the town and the valley. A popular local recreation area is Granite Dells, 4 miles north of town on US 89, which has fantastic rock formations and a fishing lake.

Besides Oak Creek Canyon (see tomorrow's Sightseeing Highlights), the Sedona area has many wonderful lessknown places to experience the wonders of the Red Rock Country. Jeep trails beckon to mountain bikers, and bikes can be rented at several shops in town. Tours by bicycle, four-wheel-drive vehicle, van, or hot-air balloon are available from numerous guide services.

Some of Sedona's most popular outdoor spots are known locally as "vortexes." These places, according to local metaphysicians, ooze earth energy that enhances psychic perception, puts channelers in touch with ancient Indian spirits, attracts UFOs, and so forth. Before you scoff, see for yourself by hiking the beautiful 3-mile Boynton Canyon Trail, the most popular vortex, from Boynton Pass Road, an extension of Dry Creek Road, which leaves US 89A in West Sedona. (The other vortexes—Airport Mesa, Bell Rock, and Cathedral Rock—are easy to locate on your own, and vortex maps are available in town.)

Bookstores

General-interest independent bookstores in the Prescott-Jerome-Sedona area include:

Anchor Books, 1046 Willow Creek Road, Prescott, (928) 778-0629.

Bookends, 3040 Windsong Drive, Suite 106 Prescott Valley, (928) 772-1868.

Book Store/Gift Corner, 885 South Main Street, Cottonwood, (928) 634-2390.

The Book Loft, 175 Highway 179, Sedona, (928) 282-5173.

The Worm Book Store, 207 North Highway 89A, Sedona, (928) 282-3471.

Sedona Books & Music, 140 Coffee Pot Drive, Sedona, (928) 203-0711.

Visitors to Sedona will soon notice that most of the bookstores in town specialize in metaphysical and New Age titles, including many you're not likely to find most other places. They include:

Crystal Castle, 313 Highway 179, Sedona, (928) 282-5910.

Crystal Magic, 2978 West Highway 89A, Sedona, (928) 282-1622.

Golden Word Book Centre, 3150 West Highway 89A, Sedona, (928) 282-2688.

Itinerary Option: Supai

Shortly before Grand Canyon Caverns on old Route 66 is a turnoff marked Supai. What the sign doesn't mention is that the isolated Indian village of Supai is down in Havasu Canyon, a branch of the Grand Canyon. On the Supai road, the pavement ends 62 miles from the turnoff. Eleven miles later, at Hualapai Hilltop, the road ends, and it's another eight miles by foot trail, descending 2,000 feet, to Supai. The trail continues to Havasu Falls and the Colorado River. Consider this trek only if you're a serious hiker with plenty of extra time (at least two days) and a desire to hike into the Grand Canyon. Backpacker camping is allowed only in two tribal campgrounds ($10) along Havasu Creek. Supai has a café, a food store, and a post office as well as a lodge ($60 double). You must pay the tribe a $20-per-person entrance fee upon arrival in Supai. Reservations are essential, even for camping. Contact Havasupai Tourist Enterprise, PO Box 160, Supai, AZ 86435, (928) 448-2121.

Flagstaff

Flagstaff, just 2½ highway hours from Phoenix and 1½ hours from Grand Canyon Village on the South Rim, is northern Arizona's tourist hub. Don't bother moving your campsite or changing motel rooms. Within a few minutes' drive from the city are enough unusual and enjoyable attractions to fill your whole day and then some.

The largest city on I 40 between Albuquerque, New Mexico, and Bakersfield, California, Flagstaff (pop. 50,000) was founded in 1881 as a railroad town (the railroad actually reached Flagstaff in 1882). The University of Northern Arizona strikes a cultural counterpoint to Flagstaff's tourist-and-truck-stop aspect.

Historic downtown Flagstaff is at the extreme west end of town. Don't be put off by the trackside heavy industry you see from the interstate or the motel-strip business route. Flagstaff's old downtown area, between Humphreys and Agassiz streets due north of the railroad station on Historic Route 66, is a low-key, low-priced, and generally underrated historic district.

Suggested Schedule

9:00 a.m.	Breakfast in Sedona.
10:00 a.m.	See Oak Creek Canyon.
Noon	Lunch in Flagstaff.
1:15 p.m.	Lowell Observatory (1:30 tour).
3:00 p.m.	Ride the chairlift at the Snowbowl.
5:00 p.m.	Check into your Flagstaff lodging if you haven't already done so.
6:00 p.m.	Dinner.

Travel Route: Sedona to Flagstaff (27 miles)

From Sedona, US 89A continues up Oak Creek Canyon as the highway climbs by sweeping curves to a usually crowded overlook on the canyon rim. From there, US 89A takes you across onto the pine-clad Coconino Plateau and, in a few minutes, into Flagstaff.

Sightseeing Highlights

Oak Creek Canyon—The scenic, very popular 27-mile canyon drive from Sedona to Flagstaff climbs from red rock desert to cool ponderosa forest. In July and August as well as early October (autumn colors), don't expect to find a parking place in any of the canyon's picnic areas or campgrounds.

Slide Rock State Park, midway up the canyon on your left, has traditionally been the local "beach" for students from the University of Northern Arizona in Flagstaff. Now a state park, it has become a little more regulated, not quite as wild as before but just as wet. The creek flows through a series of large, placid pools and down thrilling

62

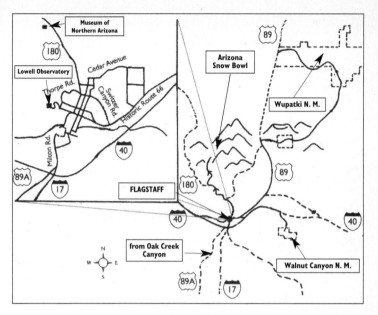

Flagstaff

spillways, flanked by a flat red sandstone shoreline where sunbathers can stretch out. Also in the park is an abandoned 1920s homestead with apple orchards. Picking the fruit is prohibited, but cider made from the apples is sold at a stand near the swimming area. The park is open during daylight hours. Admission is $5 per vehicle for up to four people over age 12, $1 per additional adult, $1 for children ages 12 and under.

Lowell Observatory—Follow winding Mars Hill Road from the west end of Historic Route 66 up to this hilltop observatory, founded by wealthy Boston businessman-turned-astronomer Percival Lowell in 1894, just 13 years after Flagstaff became a town. Lowell is best remembered for "discovering" the (nonexistent) canals of Mars and hypothesizing an ancient Martian civilization. One may wonder whether Indian ruins around Flagstaff helped guide his vivid imagination. Based on Lowell's theoretical predictions of a ninth planet, Dr. Clyde Tombaugh discovered Pluto from this observatory in 1930. The "red shift" of galaxies, on which the theory of the expanding universe is based, was also discovered here. Lowell's original telescope in its old wooden observatory tower looks like an antique left over from a Victorian science fiction novel, ideal for Martian-watching. The visitors center is open daily from 9:00 a.m. to 5:00 p.m. April through October. Tours start at 10:00 a.m. and 1:30 p.m. June through September, 1:30 p.m. only the rest of the year. Admission is $4 for adults, $3.50 for seniors, $2 for college students, and $2 for children and students under age 18. You can look through the 24-inch refracting telescope on any night—call (928) 774-2096 for prerecorded information.

Museum of Northern Arizona—This museum, located 3 miles north of downtown Flagstaff on US 180, houses one of the most comprehensive archaeology, ethnology, geology, biology, and fine arts collections in the Southwest. In July, the annual Hopi and Navajo Craftsman Exhibitions draw visitors and collectors from all over the United States. The museum is open daily from 9:00 a.m. to 5:00 p.m. Admission is $5 for adults, $4 for seniors, $3 for college students and $2 for children and students ages 7 to 17. 3101 North Fort Valley Road, (928) 774-2096.

Arizona Snow Bowl—In the San Francisco Peaks, this is the state's highest and best winter downhill ski area and a popular summer hiking trailhead. In the summer months, the chair lift carries sightseers to the summit of Mt. Humphries (11,500 ft.) for a spectacular view of Flagstaff, Sunset Crater/Wupatki, the surrounding forest and volcano fields, and the Grand Canyon in the distance. Follow US 180 for 7 miles north from Flagstaff, then turn right and go another 7 miles on an unpaved road. The lift operates daily from 10:00 a.m. until 4:00 p.m. in the summer months, and only Friday, Saturday, and Sunday in September and October. Tickets cost $9 for adults, $6.50 for seniors (free over age 70), $5 for children ages 8 to 12.

Walnut Canyon National Monument—Just 3 miles off the interstate from exit 204 east of town, Walnut Canyon offers a 1-hour walk on a paved trail around an "island" above the canyon to see about a hundred small 800-year-old cliff dwellings of the Sinagua Indians. Look-but-don't-touch views of the pristine wooded canyon floor enhance the experience. Open 8:00 a.m. to 6:00 p.m. in summer, 8:00 a.m. to 5:00 p.m. in spring and fall, and 9:00 a.m. to 5:00 p.m. the rest of the year. Admission is $3 per person, children and students under age 17 free.

Lodging

Hours from any other sizable town on Interstate 40, Flagstaff is a natural overnight stop for motorists. Cruise the 3-mile I 40 business loop north of downtown, which is lined with motels, and pick the place that appeals to you. Marquees on many motels advertise price ranges (like $50–$85); the actual room rate can change from night to night, and rooms cost about twice as much in summer as in winter. "No vacancy" problems are unlikely as long as you arrive in Flagstaff by 6:00 p.m.

Calling ahead for reservations is a good idea at "brand-name" motels such as the moderately priced **Super 8**, $40 to $75, 3725 North Kaspar Avenue, (928) 526-0818, and **Howard Johnson Inn**, $35 to $75, 3300 East Historic Route 66, (928) 526-1826, or more expensive motor inns such as the **Radisson Woodlands Hotel**, $100 to $120, 1175 West Route 66, (928) 773-8888, **Little America**, $80 to $130, 2515 East Butler Avenue, (928) 779-2471, and **Embassy Suites**, $125 to $210, 706 South Milton Street, (928) 774-4333. A plethora of independent ma-and-pa motels offer much lower rates, typically $30 to $40 double, and reservations are usually not necessary.

The last of the historic old railroad hotels in downtown Flagstaff, the **Hotel Monte Vista** at 100 North San Francisco Street, (928) 774-6971, offers guest rooms re-modeled in 1927 decor. Rates range from $50 to $120 double.

What most Flagstaff motels and motor inns share is proximity to the railroad tracks, where freight trains regularly rumble through town in the middle of the night. A pleasant alternative is to stay in one of the bed-and-breakfasts in Victorian-era homes in the turn-of-the-century residential district just north of downtown. Among them are the **Inn at 410**, 410 North Leroux Street, $135 to $190, (928) 774-0088, a Craftsman home built in 1894 for a territorial attorney general; **Lynn's Inn**, $90 to $110, 614 West Santa Fe, (928) 226-1488, an unusual 1902 mansion built of hand-quarried sandstone; the **Aspen Inn**, $80 to $100, 218 North Elden Street, (928) 773-0295; and the **Birch Tree Inn**, 824 West Birch Avenue, $70 to $120, (928) 774-1042, a former fraternity house built in 1917 with a columned portal porch and a hot tub in the garden gazebo.

Food

Flagstaff locals agree that the best place in town for fine Continental dining in an intimate atmosphere is the pricy **Cottage Place,** a 1909 bungalow two blocks south of downtown at 126 West Cottage Avenue, open Tuesday through Sunday for dinner, closed Monday, (520) 774-8431.

While every roadside chain restaurant and fast-food franchise in America is represented along Flagstaff's food and lodging strip, the most interesting thing about the dining scene here is the phenomenal number of budget- to moderate-priced Chinese restaurants. Among them are the **Grand Canyon Cafe,** 110 East Historic Route 66, (928) 774-9642; the **Mandarin Garden,** 3518 East Route 66, (928) 526-5033; the **China House Café,** 2116 East Historic Route 66, (928) 774-9824; the **Szechuan Restaurant,** 1451 South Milton Road, (928) 774-8039; the **August Moon Chinese Restaurant,** 1300 South Milton Road, (928) 774-5280; and the **China Garden Restaurant,** 1301 South Milton Road, (928) 779-0628.

Other ethnic cuisines are represented at **El Charro,** 409 South San Francisco, (928) 779-0552 (Guadalajara-style Mexican); the **Delhi Palace,** 2700 Woodlands Village Boulevard, (928) 556-0019 (East Indian); **Hassib's,** 211 South San Francisco, (928) 774-1037 (Middle Eastern); and the **Down Under Restaurant,** 6 East Aspen Avenue #100, (928) 774-6677 (New Zealand).

Camping

To reach Coconino National Forest's Bonito Campground, across from the visitors center at the south boundary of Sunset Crater, take the third Flagstaff exit

(#201) and turn north on US 89. Go 10 miles to the turnoff for Sunset Crater National Monument. Bonito Campground is on your left at the monument boundary, across the road from the Sunset Crater visitors center.

The campground is large, popular, and remarkably spacious. It often fills by 6:00 p.m., so stake out your campsite early, before taking the Sunset Crater-Wupatki drive. Sites cost $10. Volunteers from the National Monument present campfire talks nightly during the summer months. From the upper end of the campground, you can easily walk a mile or more over the cinder fields along the edge of the jagged lava flow, finding several good views of the lava and of O'Leary Crater. An unpaved road starts just east of the campground and goes 5 miles to the summit of the volcano.

Hiking and Biking

The San Francisco Peaks have a well-developed trail network. Favorite hikes in the area are two trails to the top of Mount Elden: The 2-mile **Elden Lookout Trail** up the east face from the Peaks Ranger Station, 5075 North US 89, (928) 526-0866, and the 6-mile **Oldham Trail** up the west face from the trailhead in Flagstaff's Buffalo Park. The 3-mile **Pipeline Trail** connects the two for a great all-day loop hike.

Flagstaff being a college town, bicycles are everywhere, and the city has a paved 8-mile network of biking and jogging trails. Maps are available at the Chamber of Commerce in the old downtown railroad depot. For more ambitious mountain bike tours, the favorite area is the volcano fields of **Coconino National Forest**. Check at the

Peaks Ranger Station for current route recommendations or get suggestions from any of the numerous bike rental shops in town, such as **Absolute Bikes**, 18 North San Francisco Street, (928) 779-5969, or **Mountain Sports**, 1800 South Milton Road, (928) 779-5156.

Nightlife

For its size, Flagstaff has a lot of after-dark activities, both cultural and otherwise. Most performing arts events are held at the Coconino Center for the Arts, 2300 N. Fort Valley Road, (928) 779-6921, or the Northern Arizona Univer-sity School of Performing Arts, (928) 523-3731. Local performance groups include the Flagstaff Symphony Orchestra, the Coconino Chamber Ensemble, the Flagstaff Master Chorale, the Flagstaff Oratorio Chorus, and the NAU Opera Theatre. For current infor-mation, ask at the Flagstaff Visitors Center or tune your radio to the university station, KNAU 88.7 FM.

The hottest saloon in town is the **Museum Club**, 3404 Historic Route 66, (928) 526-9434. Better known among locals as the "Zoo Club" (for reasons that will quickly become apparent), the building used to be a trading post and taxidermy shop in Flagstaff's early days and has oper-ated as a night club continuously since 1936. Live music here is country and western, and quite a few legends of country music—Bob Wills and the Texas Playboys, Willie Nelson, Commander Cody and the Lost Planet Airmen—have graced the Museum Club's stage.

Bookstores

You can still find the personal touch of independent bookstores in Flagstaff at:

Arcadia Bookstore, 116 West Cottage Avenue, (928) 779-3817.

Book Nest, 2098 North 4th Street, (928) 714-1167.

College Store, 600 Riordan Road, (928) 774-4542.

Northern Arizona University Bookstore, NAU Campus, South San Francisco Street, (928) 523-6682.

The Hopi Mesas

As long as your plans include visiting the North Rim of the Grand Canyon later in your trip, I recommend skipping the South Rim for reasons stated below. This afternoon's trip will take you to one of the earth's loneliest corners—the traditional mesa-top villages of the Hopi, who have lived there since the peak of the Anasazi civilizations at Chaco and Mesa Verde. When other Anasazi groups abandoned their desert pueblos and moved to the Rio Grande Valley, the Hopi stayed. The mesa contains an underground aquifer that has sustained the Hopi people's small, sandy fields—separate patches for red, white, blue, and yellow corn, all planted 18 inches deep—for a thousand years. The most remote of the Pueblo people, they were less influenced by missionaries than other ancient communities like Acoma were. As recently as the end of World War II, when the first school was built at Keams Canyon, no Hopi spoke English. About that time, curious scientists, writers, artists, photographers, and sightseers began visiting the Hopi mesas, sometimes disrupting kachina and snake dances until finally outsiders were banned from most Hopi ceremonies.

Hopi villagers have a way of making sightseers feel invisible. This is not hostility; it's just a helpful tool for maintaining an 11th-century agrarian culture in modern times. You can drive to most of the villages and wander freely. If you're interested in buying pottery, women who make and sell it may let you look inside their studios. All photography and sketching is strictly prohibited.

Suggested Schedule

9:00 a.m.	After breakfast, leave Flagstaff north-bound on US 89.
9:30 a.m.	Visit Sunset Crater and Wupatki national monuments.
11:00 a.m.	Continue north to Cameron, then turn east to Tuba City. Both old-time trading posts have decent restaurants for lunch.
2:30 p.m.	Reaching the Hopi mesas, visit the Hopi Cultural Center and take a tour of Walpi.
4:00 p.m.	Check into your lodging on Second Mesa. Eat dinner. After dark, stroll the mesa and listen to the silence.

Travel Route: Flagstaff to Second Mesa (113 miles)

From I 40 on the eastern edge of Flagstaff, turn north on US 89. Go 10 miles to the turnoff for Sunset Crater National Monument. From Sunset Crater, a 36-mile road takes you north to the Wupatki visitors center and then through Wupatki National Monument.

Rejoining US 89, turn right and go north for about 36 miles, then turn east on US 160. Ten miles will bring you to Tuba City. Turn south there on AZ 264. A 57-mile drive will bring you to Oraibi, westernmost of the Hopi mesa villages, on Third Mesa. Continue on the same roller-coaster highway to the Hopi Cultural Center on Second Mesa.

Sightseeing Highlights

Sunset Crater National Monument—Thousand-foot-tall Sunset Crater is the most impressive of about a dozen volcano cones that dot the forest north of Flagstaff and west of San Francisco Peaks. These volcanoes are remarkable because they are so new. Sunset Crater began erupting in the winter of 1064-65 and continued to spew cinders for almost two centuries until 1250, just an eyeblink ago in geological time. Today, scientists and tourists alike watch in suspense for rare, foreboding rumbles on the seismograph in the visitors center.

Sunset Crater is no longer very accessible to hikers. The volcano cone itself is closed to hiking (increased tourist traffic made too many unsightly footprints across the cinders); an ice cave, which was the second-best attraction, collapsed a few years ago. Today, only a short nature trail is open for walking. From the visitors center, rangers guide an assortment of other hikes as well as jeep trips up nearby O'Leary Crater outside the monument. Open daily from 8:00 a.m. to 5:00 p.m. Combined admission to Sunset Crater and Wupatki national monuments is $3 per person, children and students under 17 free.

Wupatki National Monument—Farming Indians who lived in pithouses here in the 11th century abandoned the area when Sunset Crater began to erupt. When the fireworks stopped, the porous volcanic ash retained water for better farming. Indians from several cultures—Kayenta

Anasazi, Sinagua, Hohokam, and Coconino—resettled the area. The assortment of architecture and artifacts found within just a few miles is an archaeologist's field day.

Grand Canyon National Park: South Rim—I no longer recommend visiting the South Rim of the Grand Canyon when touring the Southwest. Extreme overcrowding and a steep entrance fee have become serious problems here. You can expect to wait in an unbelievably long line of vehicles at the entrance gate. The admission fee is $20 per vehicle. Your fee receipt from the North Rim, if paid within the last seven days, will get you into the South Rim as well. Once inside the park, you will immediately be directed to one of several large parking lots, and from there a shuttle will take you to the new transportation center, where other shuttles can take you to trailheads, overlooks and museums. You can still take your own car on East Rim Drive, which leads to the east entrance, but don't count on finding a parking space at any of the scenic vistas along the way. Still, this is one of the most visited places in the national park system, so of course most motorists will want to see the South Rim for themselves in spite of the crowds. If you go, here's what to expect.

Coming from Sunset Crater and Wupatki, you will enter the park through the less-used gates at the east end of East Rim Drive. On the way to Grand Canyon Village, you will see a replica Hopi watchtower and several well-marked points with spectacular views. Take time to stop at the Tusayan ruin and museum a few miles past the watchtower to learn about the Grand Canyon's Anasazi past, as well as the Yavapai Museum, just before you reach the village, for geology and natural history exhibits. Both are free, open daily from 8:00 a.m. to 6:00 p.m. in the summer months and 9:00 a.m. to 5:00 p.m. the rest of the year. The main visitors center, just past the Yavapai Museum, is open from 8:00 a.m. to 7:00 p.m. during the summer months, until 5:00 p.m. the rest of the year.

Grand Canyon Village is big, congested with visitors, and crammed with concessionaires; the rest of the canyon rim is untouched by development. The West Rim Drive is closed to private vehicles during the summer months but accessible by free park service shuttle buses. The easy, paved South Rim Nature Trail runs 3½ miles along the rim between the Yavapai Museum, the hotel area, and the Powell Memorial on West Rim Drive.

The South Rim is most famous for its muleback trips down Bright Angel Trail. The trips are as popular as ever—so popular, in fact, that they are often booked up as much as a year in advance. To make reservations, contact Reservations Department, Grand Canyon National Park Lodges, P.O. Box 699, Grand Canyon, AZ 86023, (928) 638-2401. The cost is $70 per person, including lunch, for the one-day trip midway down the canyon, or $219 per person for an overnight trip to Phantom Ranch down on the river. Those who didn't plan that far ahead can check with the lodge to see if cancellations have created space on the next day's mule trip. You can walk over to the corral and watch the mule trips leave each morning around 9:00 to 9:30 and return around 4:30 or 5:00. You can also hike a portion of the Bright Angel Trail yourself. Take water. If you hike down this trail in the morning, you may face hot temperatures on the strenuous climb back up.

Just in case seeing the real thing isn't enough, an IMAX (semidome wraparound screen) theater in Tusayan near the main entrance gate, 7 miles south of Grand Canyon

Village, shows a half-hour film that includes rafting and flying footage. Not to be outdone, the Galaxy 4 theaters just up the road show four different Grand Canyon movies in separate viewing areas. Admission to either place is $7 ($4 for children under 12).

The Hopi Mesas—The Hopis, some of the most traditional and secretive native people of the United States, live in a series of 14 independent villages, each with fewer than 1,000 residents, above and below the rims of three high mesas. They consider themselves to be the most direct descendents of the Southwest's ancient Anasazi or Ancestral Puebloan people. Their elaborate religious ceremonies attracted so much curiosity from non-Indian sightseers in the mid- to late 20th century that today outsiders are barred from most dances, and only a few stops offer insights into Hopi ways.

On Third Mesa, **Old Oraibi** has still-occupied homes that date back to about 1125, making it the oldest continuously inhabited community in the United States. The village is often off-limits to the public, but at other unpredictable times, visitors are admitted for a small fee.

On Second Mesa, at the **Hopi Cultural Center**, you'll find excellent exhibits on Hopi customs and crafts; (928) 734-6650. The center is open Monday through Friday from 8:00 a.m. to 5:00 p.m, Saturday and Sunday from 9:00 a.m. to 3:00 p.m. MST. (The Hopi Nation, like the rest of Arizona, does not observe Daylight Savings Time; the Navajo Nation does, along with neighboring New Mexico, making it an hour ahead of Hopi time from April through October). Admission is $3 for adults, $1 for children under 13. The fixed-price Hopi arts and crafts shops nearby are good places to buy quality work. Shungopavi,

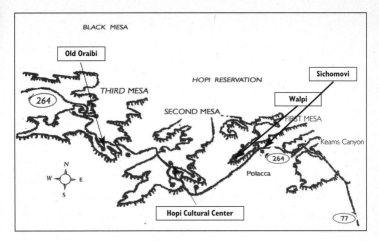

Hopi Mesas

the tribal religious center, and the smaller Second Mesa villages Shipaulovi and Mishongnovi, were all built around 1700 by people who had formerly lived below the mesa. The ruins of a previous village, Maseeba, can be seen from a Shungopavi overlook. Polacca is a 20th-century village.

Walpi, on the tip of First Mesa, dates back to about 1400. Motor vehicles are not allowed in Walpi, and outsiders can only visit the ancient town in the company of a Hopi guide. Two 18th-century villages, Sichomovi and Hano—the latter formed by immigrant Pueblo people who fled from New Mexico after the Pueblo Revolt of 1680—are suburbs of Walpi. Drive to the top of the Mesa and park in Sichomovi, then check in at the community center where you can get a guide to take you to Walpi.

Lodging

The motel at the **Hopi Cultural Center,** Box 67, Second Mesa, (928) 734-2401, has modern rooms with cable TV at about $70 double. It's the only accommodation on the Hopi Mesas, so reservations are recommended. If you decide to visit the South Rim of the Grand Canyon along the way, there are plenty of hotel choices. Reservations are essential at any of them most of the year. The original hotel built on the rim of the Grand Canyon by Fred Harvey in 1905, **El Tovar** is still the most elegant of the several hotels in Grand Canyon Village. Room rates are from $126 to $294. Also on the rim are **Kachina Lodge**, $124 to $134, **Yavapai Lodge**, $92 to $106, and **Maswik Lodge**, $63 to $123. Check-in time at all of the Grand Canyon Village lodges is 3:30. Reservations should be made far in advance through Grand Canyon National Park Lodges, P.O. Box 699, Grand Canyon, AZ 86023, (303) 297-2757 or www.grandcanyonlodges.com.

If you arrive without reservations and find no vacancies within the park, there is a cluster of large resort motels just outside the south entrance. Prices are pretty much the same as at the Grand Canyon Village lodges, and the view isn't as nice.

Food

The restaurant at the Hopi Cultural Center, the only one on the reservation, features traditional Hopi dishes such as lamb stew, bean soup, and blue corn pancakes. Open daily from 6:30 a.m. to 9:00 p.m. in the summer months, until 8:00 p.m. the rest of the year.

Grand Canyon Village has restaurant concessionaires in all price ranges. The main dining room at **El Tovar** serves Continental cuisine nightly from 5:00 to 10:00 p.m. as well as breakfast (6:30 to 11:00 a.m.) and luncheon (11:30 a.m.

to 2:00 p.m.). There is also a steak house, a hamburger restaurant, a snack bar, and a campers' grocery store.

Camping

Camp on the Hopi Reservation at the free **Second Mesa Campground and Trailer Park** next to the Cultural Center. You won't find water or hookups, but you can use the rest rooms and other services at the center. Other campgrounds are located below the mesas at Keams Canyon and at Kykotsmovi, a mile east of New Oraibi.

To stay in the campground at Grand Canyon Village, you must make reservations (at least a month in advance) by calling (800) 365-2267 or contacting http://reservations.nps.gov and prepaying your camping fee with your Visa or MasterCard. Fees start at $10. There are private campgrounds outside the main gate, 7 miles south of Grand Canyon Village.

Hiking and Biking

Hiking and biking are not permitted on the Hopi Reservation, and there are an extraordinary number of tribal police around to enforce such rules. On the Navajo Reservation, hikers or bikers planning to leave the main roads must first obtain a permit from the tribal administrative offices in Window Rock or Tuba City.

The South Rim of the Grand Canyon offers dozens of hiking possibilities. The easy, paved **South Rim Nature Trail** runs more than 3 miles along the rim between the Yavapai Museum, the hotel area, and the Powell Memorial on West Rim Drive.

For a more ambitious hike, join the parade of trekkers on the **Bright Angel Trail,** a 10-mile (one-way) trip from the rim to the river 4,800 feet below. If you plan to spend the night in the canyon, you must obtain a free back-country permit from the visitors center first. The round-trip to the bottom of the canyon and back can be done in a single day only if you start well before dawn and make the return trip by moonlight. A more reasonable one-day hike on the Bright Angel Trail is to Plateau Point, 1,300 feet above the river and just before the grueling final descent. Hiking into the canyon on a summer morning, you can expect very hot temperatures on the strenuous climb back up.

Two shorter, steeper, less-used trails—the **South Kaibab Trail** (7 miles to the river) and the **Grandview Trail** (3 miles to Tonto Trail; does not reach the river)—go down into the canyon from overlooks along East Rim Drive, and two others—the **Hermit Trail** (9 miles to the river) and the **Boucher Trail** (11 miles to the Tonto Trail)—start from West Rim Drive. All trails into the canyon intersect the **Tonto Trail,** a 92-mile former mining road that parallels the rim midway down the canyon wall, making it possible to hike down by one route and return by another.

Beyond the Petrified Forest

This long driving day will take you through the painted desert country of eastern Arizona, then back to New Mexico in the land of the Zuni. This afternoon, visit a place where every expedition that passed through New Mexico for 200 years left its mark in stone alongside petroglyphs of the Anasazi before them. Later on, see the volcano fields of El Malpais or take a late afternoon side trip to Acoma, the most beautiful of all Indian pueblos.

Suggested Schedule

8:00 a.m.	Get an early start. You may wish to wait until you reach Holbrook to eat breakfast.
10:00 a.m.	Visit Petrified Forest National Park. Take a short hike.
Noon	Drive across the Zuni lands to El Morro National Monument.
2:30 p.m.	Visit El Morro National Monument.
3:30 p.m.	Drive on to Bandera Crater in El Malpais National Monument.

4:00 p.m. Climb up the volcano and down into the ice cave.

5:30 p.m. Check into your motel in Grants (or drive on to Albuquerque).

Travel Route: Second Mesa to Grants (325 miles)

Continue on AZ 264 over First Mesa, through Keams Canyon, a total distance of 39 miles to the turnoff for Tribal Route 6, which becomes AZ 77 and goes to Holbrook, 59 miles to the south. There are no towns along this route. You will reach I 40 just east of Holbrook. After stopping in town for gasoline if necessary, proceed eastbound on I 40 for 25 miles to the Petrified Forest National Park entrance.

After the 27-mile drive through the Petrified Forest, exit at the far end of the park on US 180 and drive 36 miles east across empty, arid rangeland to St. Johns. Turn north on US 191 and drive north for 29 miles to the turnoff for AZ 61 on your right. A few miles east, AZ 61 changes into NM 53. Stay on that road, admiring the pink cliffs of the Zuni Mountains, for 30 miles to the town of Zuni and about 40 more miles to El Morro National Monument.

As you continue east on NM 53 for the 40-mile drive from El Morro National Monument to Grants, watch for the little road on your right to Bandera Crater and Ice Cave, near where the highway crosses the crest of the mountains. Several miles farther along, a big brown National Park Service sign marks the trailhead for the Zuni-Acoma Trail.

NM 53 brings you back to I 40 at the western Grants/Milan exit. To see the other side of El Malpais, with the

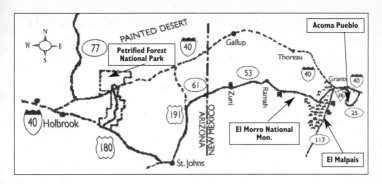

Holbrook to Grants

best views of the lava fields, take either the interstate or the business loop to the eastern Grants exit and follow NM 117 south for 10 miles to Sandstone Bluff Overlook and 7 more miles to La Ventana Natural Arch. Return to the interstate by the same route.

The exit to Acoma is 15 miles east on I 40. Albuquerque is another 60 miles down the interstate. (If you will be driving on to Albuquerque tomorrow morning, wait until then to visit Acoma. If you plan to spend tonight in Albuquerque, consider skipping something else on today's itinerary to make time to visit this magnificent, ancient town.

Sightseeing Highlights

Petrified Forest National Park—This colorful patch of apparent wasteland was a tropical forest 200 million years ago. Trees similar to California's giant redwoods grew along the shore of a sea that rose and receded over countless millennia to deposit multicolored layers of sediment, burying and petrifying parts of the forest. Wind and rain erosion have exposed the huge stone tree trunks and created the striking painted desert around them. The idea of primeval forest here, in a land where today scraggly clumps of grass struggle to survive, challenges the imagination. With the coming of the railroad in 1883, entrepreneurs began sawing and polishing petrified wood to ship back east, where it was a fashionable material for table tops. In just 16 years, they shipped out over 20 million pounds of it. To stop the plunder, Theodore Roosevelt declared the petrified forest a national monument in 1899. It was raised to national park status in 1962. The National Park Service is very serious about preventing the removal of petrified wood, and vehicles are subject to search by rangers on the way out.

The most extensive petrified forest areas are in the southern part of the park. Along the 27-mile scenic drive from the south gate on US 180 to the north gate on I 40, stop and walk through the strange landscape near the Rainbow Forest Museum and at the Crystal Forest and Jasper Forest turnouts. Take the three-quarter-mile paved walking trail among blue, white, and brown striped hills from the fourth turnout on the one-way loop road at Blue Mesa, midway through the park.

The park is open only during daylight hours. Admission is $10 per vehicle. There is no lodge or campground. Food, gasoline, and souvenirs, including lots of petrified wood imported from outside the park (keep your receipt until you leave the park), are sold at the Painted Desert Oasis by the visitors center at the north gate.

Zuni Reservation—The people who live here are classified as Pueblo Indians, although their language is not related to that of any other known Native American tribe. They are best known for the costumed Shalako house-blessing ceremonies held around the beginning of December. Now mostly of modern construction, the town of Zuni has been continuously occupied for 700 years. Ancient ruins around Zuni were to become Zuni-Cibola National Historic Park under a resolution passed by the U.S. Congress in 1988. Unfortunately, nobody consulted the Zuni people about it until 1990, when they voted the plan down. The ruins remain closed to the non-Indian public. Although it has no national park, the reservation does have some pretty little fishing lakes.

El Morro National Monument—America's first national monument (1906), El Morro was established to protect the many inscriptions scratched into the sandstone around a lovely oasis at the base of the 200-foot cliffs. Though wading and bathing are prohibited, the pool looks so inviting that it's no mystery why just about every southwestern expedition for three centuries stopped here. (Besides, it was the only water for miles around.) Observe how many Spanish conquistadors, *whowrotewithoutspacesbetween words*, recorded that their journeys were "a su cuesta" (at their own expense), and note the tombstonelike precision with which U.S. military explorers inscribed their graffiti. The earliest Spanish inscription (1605) is that of Don Juan de Oñate, who led the first settlers to New Mexico. Native American petroglyphs on the same rock are twice as old.

The best part of a visit to El Morro is the one-hour loop hike to the top of the rock, where you'll find the ruins of a small Anasazi pueblo with a magnificent view. Surprise: the cliff that looks so solid and massive from below is actually a wall, 200 feet high but just a few feet thick, separating the visitors center area from a box canyon.

The visitors center and trail are open daily from 8:00 a.m. to 7:00 p.m. in the summer months, until 5:00 p.m.

the rest of the year. Admission is $4 per vehicle. While at the visitors center, pick up information sheets on nearby undeveloped El Malpais National Monument.

El Malpais National Monument and Conservation Area—Created by act of Congress in 1988, El Malpais has seen no improvements except for a few signs. The information center, at 100 Iron Street in Grants, can furnish photocopied flyers on hiking and show you a map of the area. Otherwise, you're on your own. Malpais, Spanish for "badlands," is the name given to lava beds throughout New Mexico.

Three thousand years ago, a row of volcanoes gushed a river of molten rock 30 miles long and up to 20 miles wide. You can hike along the edge of the lava beds, which are quite different from those you saw at Sunset Crater, by taking the Zuni-Acoma Trail (see Hiking and Biking later in this chapter). The best view of the lava field is from the opposite side of the lava field at Sandstone Bluff Overlook on NM 117. From there, continue to La Ventana to see the largest accessible natural arch in New Mexico.

Hike about a mile to see Bandera Crater, one of five volcanoes that created the El Malpais lava field. Nearby, another short trail leads to an ice cave. The porous lava insulates an underground pond, keeping it perpetually frozen; the cave is often 70 degrees cooler than the temperature on the surface. The only developed facility within the monument, the crater and ice caves still operate much as they did when they were a privately owned tourist attraction. Hours are 8:00 a.m. to 7:00 p.m. during the summer months, until 4:00 p.m. the rest of the year. Admission is $7 for adults, $3.50 for children ages 5 to 11.

Acoma (Sky City)—Acoma is the most impressively situated of New Mexico's Indian pueblos as well as one of the oldest and most traditional. Continuously inhabited since A.D. 1075 (when Chaco Canyon was at its zenith), Acoma was one of the towns, along with Zuni, that inspired the "Seven Cities of Cibola" legend that drew Coronado to explore the American Southwest in 1540 in search of rumored wealth surpassing that of the Incas. (Was he disappointed!) The pueblo also has a Franciscan mission church dating from 1629 (older than San Miguel, Santa Fe's "Oldest Church in the U.S."). Eighty such missions were built in the 1600s, but only two survived the Pueblo Revolt of 1680. The other is at Isleta Pueblo near Albuquerque.

While most Acoma people now live in modern villages below the mesa, the old pueblo remains the center of religious life. Acoma is on top of the 400-foot mesa, 13 miles by road from the interstate. No cars are permitted beyond the tribal visitors center. Access is by shuttle bus. The tours, which run hourly from 8:00 a.m. to 6:00 p.m. during the summer months (shorter hours off-season) cost $8 per person. There is a fee of $10 for still photography or sketching, higher for videocams. The pueblo is closed for religious ceremonies to which the public is not invited on several days during the summer and fall. For current schedule information, call ahead at (505) 252-1139.

Lodging

The closest motel accommodations are one hour's drive beyond El Morro at the town of Grants on I 40. A faded uranium mining center of the 1950s, Grants exists today mainly as an overnight stop for trucks, and motel prices are low enough to convince big-rig drivers to stay here instead of rolling on into Albuquerque. Top of the line is **The Inn & Suites of Grants**, 1501 East Santa Fe Avenue, (505) 287-7901, with in-room movies, a whirlpool and sauna, and a café; doubles start at about $70. In the moderate price range, the **Sands Motel**, 112 McArthur Street, (505) 287-2991, has doubles for $42 and up and a location off the main thoroughfare. There are also about a dozen ma-and-pa motels where you can get a decent room for about $30. If you're camping your way across the Southwest on a budget, you won't find a cheaper shower, real bed, and cable color TV anywhere. Look at the room first and make sure the plumbing and TV work.

Another lodging possibility in the area is the new **Sky City Hotel & Conference Center**, located beside the Sky City Casino at the Acoma exit 15 miles east of Grants on Interstate 25. Rooms range from $60 for standard doubles to $125 for luxury suites. (505) 552-6123.

Food

There is a restaurant at Petrified Forest National Park but none at El Morro. In fact, except for a small café in Zuni, there is no food to be found along this afternoon's route. If you're camping, stock up on groceries in Holbrook or St. Johns. Otherwise, the only restaurants around are in Grants. After trying most of the family restaurants, fast-food joints, and other dining possibilities around Grants, the best food I've found is at the salad bar in the **Iron Skillet Restaurant** (505-285-6621) at the Petro Stopping Center, the truck stop 3 miles west of town at the Milan exit from I 40. In case you want to place a collect or credit card phone call home, there is a telephone at each table. There are also pay showers, video games, a pay computer where you can check your e-mail, and a store that sells cowboy hats, boots, huge belt buckles, auto repair tools, CB radios, portable sound systems, C&W cassettes, paper-back westerns, soft drinks, beef jerky, silly postcards, the latest in radar detection technology—everything an inter-state trucker needs.

Another good place to eat in the area is the all-you-can-eat buffet inside the **Sky City Casino**, just off the interstate 15 miles east of Grants. Unfortunately, they serve breakfast only on Saturday (8:30 to 10:30 a.m.); lunch (11:30 a.m. to 4:30 p.m.) and dinner (5:00 to 9:30 p.m.) daily, plus Sunday brunch (10:30 a.m. to 4:30 p.m.). (505) 552-6017.

Camping

El Morro National Monument has a small, pleasant campground among the juniper trees. It only fills up on weekends. There is no camping fee, though a donation box quietly solicits voluntary contributions to help pay for the new restroom.

In case you find the El Morro campground full, go to the **Inscription Rock RV Park** about a mile farther along New Mexico 53. Sites run $17 with full hookups, $10 without.

Hiking and Biking

To discover the uniquenesss of El Malpais National Monu-ment, take the **Zuni-Acoma Trail**, a fragment of the route that once linked the two ancient pueblos.

Although mostly level, it is slow and difficult because of the rough terrain. The trail itself is indistinct, so you must follow marker posts. The marked portion of the trail runs for 7½ miles, but the first mile may be enough.

Mountain bikers in the Grants area head for **Mount Taylor,** the 11,301-foot mountain just north of town. A well-maintained forest road, paved partway, leads to the top ridge, where there are a number of good backcountry rides including a closed-to-vehicles road that leads to an old fire lookout near the summit.

Bookstores

Booksellers, like other folks, are few and far between in these parts. Try:

Front Row Seat, 700 E. Roosevelt Avenue, Grants, (505) 285-5900.

Albuquerque

At the crossroads of two interstate highways and with the state's only major commercial airport, Albuquerque anchors the eastern edge of the Southwest. Like Las Vegas, it is a new city in an ancient land. Before World War II, Albuquerque was a sleepy little university town about the same size as Santa Fe. Its strategic location at the intersection of I 25 and I 40 explains why Albuquerque and its suburbs have surpassed half a million in population, while other New Mexican towns remain small.

All streets are designated by quadrant. For example, if you're on Lomas Boulevard NE, you are north of Central Avenue (old Route 66) and east of the railroad tracks. These traditional dividing lines meet close enough to the "Big I"—the intersection of Interstates 25 and 40—so that the quadrant system will generally tell you which direction you are from both major freeways. It's hard to get lost as long as you remember that Sandia Crest, the big mountain nearby, is to the east.

You can't go far in Albuquerque without seeing the ubiquitous hot air balloon motif that is this city's claim to fame. The Kodak Albuquerque International Balloon

Fiesta, held annually in early October, is the largest event of its kind in the world, featuring mass ascensions of over 500 balloons and drawing crowds of over half a million. If the Balloon Fiesta doesn't fit into your trip schedule, you can still see anywhere from a dozen to 50 balloons floating above the city, roaring with sounds like dragon breath and sometimes bouncing off suburban rooftops, practically any sunny weekend morning. The best spot from which to watch this spectacle is the rim of West Mesa Escarpment, reached via the maze of unpaved roads to the south above Petroglyph National Monument.

Note: The telephone area code for Albuquerque, Santa Fe, and Los Alamos is scheduled to change in 2002 to 557.

Suggested Schedule

9:00 a.m.	Visit Acoma (see yesterday's Sightseeing Highlights).
10:30 a.m.	Drive to Albuquerque.
11:30 a.m.	Arrive in Albuquerque. Lunch at the Indian Pueblo Cultural Center.
1:00 p.m.	Drive up Sandia Crest or visit the zoo and aquarium.
4:00 p.m.	Visit Old Town.
6:00 p.m.	Dinner in Old Town.

A mountaintop is the ideal place to be on a hot day, but a bad place to be during a thunderstorm. If you're visiting Albuquerque in June, the hottest month of the year, plan your trip up Sandia Crest in the afternoon; if it's July or August, when storms are the norm, go in the morning.

Travel Route: Grants to Albuquerque (77 miles)

Albuquerque is 77 miles east of Grants on Interstate 40. The trip takes an hour. There is no alternative scenic route, though Indian buffs may choose to turn off at Acoma and follow old NM 124, which parallels the interstate at a distance for about 15 miles and goes through several villages on the Laguna Indian Reservation.

Sightseeing Highlights

Petroglyph National Monument—West Mesa Escarpment, the cliff below the small, extinct volcanoes on the horizon, defines the western edge of Albuquerque. Housing subdivisions sprawl up to the base of the escarpment; from the top rim, the land is empty and almost roadless for a hundred miles to the west, home only to jackrabbits and coyotes. The black volcanic boulders tumbled all along the escarpment contain over 15,000 pre-Columbian Indian petroglyphs—more than at any other site in the United States. Much of this rock art dates back a thousand years or more.

In 1988, the federal government decided to declare a large area of the West Mesa Escarpment a national monument, but so far the funds have not been available to acquire most of the land that will eventually be included in the national monument. You can see some of the best rock art by climbing the trail through the part of the park where Atrisco Road nears the top rim of the escarpment.

The meanings of some of the petroglyphs, such as animal pictures, are self-evident, and anthropologists have interpreted some of the abstract symbols with the help of modern-day Rio Grande Pueblo people, whose ancient ancestors chipped them into the rocks. Some of the figures remain mysterious. Notice the images of Kokopelli, the hunchbacked flute player thought to symbolize fertility, which are common throughout the Anasazi country in New Mexico, Colorado, Utah, and Arizona. Humanlike horned figures may represent prehistoric shamans. Early Spanish settlers believed that they were devils and carved crosses near them to neutralize their supposed black magic powers.

To reach Petroglyph Park, take I 40 west and turn off northbound at Coors Road, exit 155. Veer left and follow Atrisco Road to the park. Free admission.

Indian Pueblo Cultural Center—Owned by the Native American Pueblos of New Mexico, this cultural center has a series of galleries selling Indian arts and crafts in all price ranges surrounding the central open-air dance plaza, as well as a museum. Indian dances and craft demonstrations are held here on most weekends during the spring, summer, and autumn months—sometimes free, other times for a small admission fee; for the current schedule of events, call (505) 843-7270. The cultural center also has a moderately priced restaurant specializing in Native American cuisine, making it an ideal lunch stop. Open daily from 9:00 a.m. to 5:30 p.m., closed Thanksgiving, Christmas, and New Year's Day. Admission to the retail galleries is free; entry to the museum costs $4 for adults, $3 for seniors over age 62, $1 for students. The center is at 2401 12th Street NW, a few blocks north of I 40 exit 157B.

Rio Grande Zoological Park—This first-rate zoo keeps more than 1,000 animals, including such oddities as piranhas and komodo dragons, in naturalistic habitats,

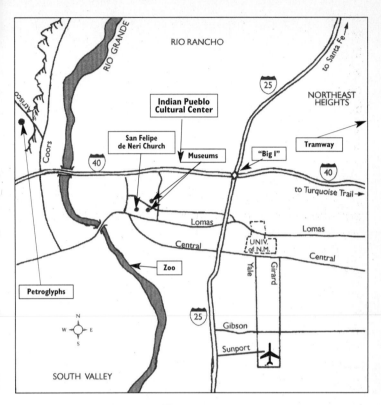

Albuquerque

including an elaborate tropical rainforest re-creation. The zoo also has the largest captive breeding program for the endangered lobo, or Mexican wolf; a program is underway to re-introduce the wolves into the wild in southwestern New Mexico, though of the small number of wolves that have been released, few have survived. Open daily except Monday from 9:00 a.m. to 5:00 p.m., to 6:00 on summer weekends; adults $4.50, seniors and children ages 3 to 15 $2.50. 903 10th Street, (505) 764-6200.

Albuquerque Aquarium—A lot of imagination went into designing this underwater oasis in the desert, focusing on the marine life and ecosystems of the Rio Grande, from its source in the Colorado Rockies to its mouth at the Gulf of Mexico. The centerpiece is a re-created shipwreck inhabited by reef life—including sharks. Cool and blue, this is the ideal place to visit on a hot day. Open daily except Monday from 9:00 a.m. to 5:00 p.m., to 6:00 p.m. on summer weekends; adults $4.50, children and students ages 3 to 15 and seniors $2.50. 2601 Central Avenue, (505) 764-6200. On the other side of the parking lot, the Rio Grande Botanic Garden has greenhouse-style conservatories of desert and Mediterranean plants, as well as a butterfly pavilion. Address, admission, and phone number information is the same as for the aquarium; combination tickets are available.

Old Town—Albuquerque's original town plaza, dating back to 1706, has remained remarkably intact as highrise buildings have sprouted up all around it in recent years, creating an oasis of antiquity in the midst of the modern city. Browse in the art galleries and shops; examine the wares of the Pueblo Indian vendors who line the sidewalks. Pause for a quiet moment in the 18th-century San Felipe de Neri Church on the northwest corner of the plaza. Free walking tours of Old Town start from the nearby Albuquerque Museum of Art & History daily except Mondays at 11:00 a.m. Old Town is one-half mile south of I 40 exit 157A via Rio Grande Boulevard.

New Mexico Museum of Natural History—Among the museum's feature attractions are full-scale dinosaur models, exhibits about New Mexico's human and animal inhabitants in the last Ice Age, and a large display about the Rio Grande, including aquariums of fish that live in the river. The most unusual and memorable of the museum's exhibits include a realistic journey into the depths of a volcano and a time machine simulation. There's also a planetarium. Open daily from 9:00 a.m. to 5:00 p.m., adults $5.25, students and senior citizens $4.20, children ages 3 to 11 $2.10; planetarium shows: adults $5, students and seniors $4, children $3. The museum is at 1801 Mountain Road NW, near Old Town. For current exhibit information, call (505) 841-2800; planetarium schedule: (505) 841-5950.

Across the road, the **Albuquerque Museum of Art & History** features an impressive permanent exhibit entitled "Four Centuries: A History of Albuquerque," containing the largest collection of Spanish colonial artifacts in the United States. Other features include a sculpture garden and children's exhibits. The museum is open daily except Monday from 9:00 a.m. to 5:00 p.m. Admission is free. The museum is at 2000 Mountain Road NW, (505) 243-7255.

And if you just can't get enough of museums, also in the Old Town area is the **American International Rattlesnake Museum**, with more than 30 kinds of rattlesnakes on display. Videos explain more than you may want to know about these reclusive symbols of the Southwestern desert, and there's even an exhibit of artworks depicting rattlesnakes. Open daily except Sunday from 10:00 a.m. to 6:00 p.m., adults $2.50, children and students ages 3 to 17 $1.50. The privately-owned museum is at 202 San Felipe Street, (505) 242-6569.

Maxwell Museum of Anthropology—This stuffy little museum on the University of New Mexico campus contains exhibits on the Athabascan (Navajo and Apache) and Anasazi cultures, with special emphasis on Chaco Canyon, and provides a good introduction to many Native American tribes and sites you will see later in this itinerary. The university is about 2 miles east of I 25 via Central Avenue; Maxwell Museum is near the west edge of the campus, two blocks north of Central on Redondo Drive. Open Monday through Friday from 9:00 a.m. to 4:00 p.m., Saturdays from 10:00 a.m. to 4:00 p.m., free. Phone (505) 277-4404 for information. The UNM campus also offers a unique Meteorite Museum with sample space rocks from all over the world. Located in the Earth and Planetary Sciences Building at 200 Yale Boulevard, it has the same hours as the anthropology museum; free. (505) 277-2747.

Spanish History Museum—Displays the colonial history of New Mexico from the travels of early conquistadores to 1912, when statehood was granted. Other exhibits reveal the roles Hispanics have played in U.S. history, such as Spanish aid to George Washington's revolutionary army. The museum is two blocks south of the University of New Mexico at 2221 Lead SE. Open daily 1:00 to 5:00 p.m. Admission is $2 per person, children under 12 free. Phone (505) 268-9981 for information.

Sandia Crest—A trip to the mountaintop is a must for visitors, not only for the spectacular view but also because temperatures on Sandia Crest average about 30 degrees cooler than downtown, offering a welcome escape from the city's midsummer afternoon heat. You can get to the summit by riding the world's longest aerial tramway or by driving the steep paved road up the back side of the mountain, a side trip from the Turquoise Trail.

To take the Sandia Peak Aerial Tramway (adults $14,

seniors and children age 5 to 12 $10), go east on I 40 to Exit 167 and follow Tramway Boulevard north for 10 miles to the base terminal. The tramway operates daily during the summer months from 9:00 a.m. to 10:00 p.m., and during spring and autumn daily from 9:00 a.m. to 9:00 p.m. weekends, to 8:00 p.m. weekdays; on Wednesday it does not begin running until 5:00 p.m.; closed during ski season. During the summer you can also get a combination ticket to ride both the tramway and the ski area chairlift on the other side of the mountain ($19 for adults, $15 for seniors and children).

To drive to the top of Sandia Crest and see the view for free, follow the Turquoise Trail (see Day 8). The steep, paved road up to Sandia Crest splits off to the left at Cedar Crest, the first town you reach on NM 14 after leaving the interstate. There is a snack bar at the auto road summit house and a more complete restaurant and bar at the tramway station.

Your itinerary for the next week lies before your eyes as you survey the 360-degree horizon from Sandia Crest. To the north, bordering the Rio Grande, the volcanic Jemez Mountains conceal Los Alamos and Bandelier National Monument (Day 9). The Sangre de Cristo Mountains to the northeast range from Santa Fe (Day 8) at the southern tip in a nearly unbroken wall of rock for 200 miles north past Taos into Colorado and beyond the Great Sand Dunes (Day 11). Far on the northern skyline, you may barely make out southwestern Colorado's San Juan Mountains, which you'll cross on your way west to Durango and Mesa Verde (Days 12 and 13). Then you'll return south through Chaco Canyon (Day 14) in the San Juan Basin, which lies between the Jemez Mountains and

Mt. Taylor, the big solitary mountain that should be clearly visible to the west, which stands near Grants.

"Sandia," by the way, means "watermelon" in Spanish.

Lodging

More than any other community in this book, the Albuquerque lodging scene is dominated by major hotel and motor inn chains. And why not? New Mexico-born hotelier Conrad Hilton got his start here. Hilton's original hotel is no longer in operation; its successor, the 12-story **Hilton Albuquerque,** is located near the University of New Mexico campus at 1901 University Boulevard NE, (505) 884-2500; room rates are $92 to $102 a night. Another towering business-style hotel, the **Sheraton Old Town** has a prime location just a short walk from Old Town Plaza with its restaurants, shopping, and historic ambience. 800 Rio Grande Boulevard NW, (505) 843-6300. Rooms costs $120 to $140 a night.

A great Albuquerque bed-and-breakfast inn near Old Town is the **Brittania & W. E. Mauger Estate,** at 701 Roma Avenue NW, (505) 242-8755. This three-story brick Queen Anne Victorian mansion, built in 1896, has eight guest rooms with antique furnishings and private baths. Room rates of $89 to $179 double include continental breakfast. Reservations are essential.

Name brand motor hotels cluster around the intersection of I 25 and Lomas Boulevard, including the **Holiday Inn-Midtown,** 2020 Menaul Boulevard NE, (505) 884-2511, doubles $100 to $110 in season, or as low as $89 off-season. Farther north on I 25 is the **Holiday Inn Pyramid Hotel at Journal Center,** 5151 San Francisco

Road NE (at exit 232), (505) 821-3333. Built in the shape of an Aztec pyramid, this hotel has a 50-foot waterfall inside its 10-story atrium lobby. Rates are $100 to $140 double. Catering primarily to businessmen, several of these hotels offer special rates on weekend nights.

Budget motels include the **Lorilodge Motel East** at 801 Central Avenue NE, just off I 25, (505) 243-2891, with doubles from $24 to $38, and the **De Anza Motel**, 4301 Central Avenue NE, (505) 255-1654, with doubles for under $30. The latter, one of a cluster of motels on what was once the east edge of town along Route 66, is in what is considered by many to be a less than desirable neighborhood.

Food

The best bet for lunch is the restaurant at the **Indian Pueblo Cultural Center** (see Sightseeing Highlights), open daily from 7:30 a.m. to 3:30 p.m. Specialties are Native American dishes such as Indian tacos, posole, and spiced bread pudding.

High on Sandia Crest, with prices to match, **High Finance** at the top of the tramway serves steaks, seafood, pasta, and Mexican food daily from 11:00 a.m. to 2:30 p.m. and 4:30 to 9:00 p.m., with barbecues on weekends. Sunset dining here makes for an incomparable experience. Guests with dinner reservations receive a discount on tram ticket prices.

Another extraordinary luxury restaurant is the **Ranchers Club** in the Albuquerque Hilton hotel, 1901 University Avenue NE, (505) 884-2500. As the name suggests, steak is the specialty here—but no ordinary steak. The menu includes a 40-ounce T-bone and a 48-ounce porterhouse. Guests can choose which wood will be used to barbecue their steaks—mesquite, hickory, sassafras, or wild cherry.

Good places to dine around Old Town include **Maria Teresa**, 618 Rio Grande Boulevard, (505) 242-3900, and **High Noon**, 425 San Felipe NW, (505) 765-1455; both are in historic buildings and specialize in New Mexican and Continental cuisine. For more moderate prices on Old Town Plaza, enjoy Mexican food at colorful **La Hacienda**, (505) 243-3131, serving from 11:00 a.m. to 9:00 p.m. daily. A still more affordable restaurant in the same area, for lunch only, is **Christopher's**, 323 Romero NW, (505) 242-0202, serving New Mexican food daily from 11:00 a.m. to 3:00 p.m.

For low-priced eating with the college crowd, especially recommended for breakfast, try the huevos rancheros (fried eggs on a tortilla, smothered in hot salsa) and giant cinnamon rolls at the **Frontier Restaurant** on Central Avenue across from the University of New Mexico campus, open daily from 6:30 a.m. to midnight.

Another unique, budget-priced restaurant in the university area is the **66 Diner**, 1405 Central Avenue NE, (505) 247-1421, a 1950s-style diner that enthusiastically promotes nostalgia for old Route 66, which ran through Albuquerque on Central Avenue before Interstate 40 was built. The chef recommends the fries, shakes, and green chile cheese dogs.

Hiking and Biking

The **Paseo del Bosque**, a paved jogging and biking trail among the cottonwoods that follows the Rio Grande for 5 miles through Albuquerque, is easily reached from the

Rio Grande Zoological Park. Another access point is the Rio Grande Nature Center State Park, 2901 Candelaria Road NW, (505) 344-7240. The trail continues as **Paseo del Noreste**, without the pavement, for 6 more miles northward toward the suburb of Rio Rancho. Along most of the Paseo route, you'd never know you were in a city were it not for the sound of air traffic. The trail is walkable, but better for biking.

An easy, mile-long walking trail along Sandia Crest between the tramway station and the auto road summit house gives you an eagle's-eye view of the city a mile below. The Crest Trail continues in both directions for a total distance of more than 20 miles through the Sandia Wilderness (no mountain bikes).

Nightlife

The University of New Mexico is the hub of Albuquerque's active performing arts sphere. On campus, **Popejoy Hall**, (505) 277-3824, hosts the Albuquerque Civic Light Opera, the New Mexico Jazz Workshop, and the New Mexico Symphony Orchestra, as well as popular music concerts. The historic **KiMo Theater**, downtown at 423 Central Avenue NE, (505) 848-1370, is the venue for performances by such groups as the Albuquerque Ballet Company, the New Mexico Repertory Company, and the unique Compania de Teatro, a repertory group that performs plays in English, Spanish, and even Northern New Mexican "Spanglish."

For live rock music, check out **The Launchpad**, downtown at 618 Central Avenue SW, (505) 764-8887. You'll find R&B at the **Club Rhythm & Blues**, 3523 Central

Avenue NE, (505) 256-0849, and C&W at the **Ranch Bar & Lounge,** 8900 Central Avenue SE, (505) 275-1616. Albuquerque's big comedy club is **Laffs,** 3100 Juan Tabo Boulevard NE, (505) 296-5653. Tuesdays are open-mike amateur nights.

There are Indian casinos just off Interstate 25 on both the northern and southern outskirts of Albuquerque. South of town is the **Isleta Gaming Palace,** 11000 Broadway SE, (505) 869-2614. On the north side is the **Sandia Casino,** Tramway Road at I 25 exit 234, (505) 897-2173. A little farther north at the town of Bernalillo is the **Santa Ana Star Casino,** 54 Jemez Canyon Dam Road, (505) 867-0000.

Bookstores

All major bookstore chains are well-represented in Albuquerque, though small "mom-and-pop" booksellers are almost extinct here. Page One and Bound to Be Read, both independent bookstores that are as large as any chain location in the city, have outstanding selections of books on all Southwestern topics.

Book Works, 4022 Rio Grande Boulevard South, (505) 344-8139.

Bound to Be Read, 6300 San Mateo Boulevard NE, (505) 828-3500.

Page One, 11018 Montgomery Boulevard NE, (505) 294-2026.

University of New Mexico Bookstore, 2301 Central Avenue NE, (505) 277-5451.

Day 8

Santa Fe

From Albuquerque, a one-hour drive will take you across the stretch of rugged mountains and high desert to the gateway of one of our nation's most isolated corners, where history has created a tricultural blend that is unique in the world. Santa Fe has been New Mexico's capital since 1610.

Northern New Mexico feels foreign, and it's no wonder. For over two centuries, New Mexico was the northernmost Spanish colony in the New World, its border closed to foreigners. It became a state of newly independent Mexico in 1821 but was demoted to Mexican territorial status in 1836, invaded by the Republic of Texas in 1841, occupied by the U.S. Army in 1846 during the Mexican War, declared U.S. territory in 1848, and unsuccessfully invaded by the Confederacy in 1862. It became a U.S. state in 1912. Which nation owned New Mexico is of little import to local residents, who believe their home is unlike anyplace else in America.

Santa Fe (pop. 60,000) prides itself on its antiquity and blend of Native American, Latino, and Anglo cultural influences. The Pueblo people have occupied the area for at least 700 years, while the Spanish arrived almost 400 years ago to establish the northernmost Spanish colony in the New World. Santa Fe's population today is about 50 percent Hispanic, and a distinctive regional dialect of Spanish is commonly spoken by New Mexicans; the city also has a fast-growing Mexican immigrant population with different customs. The capital of a culturally diverse state that also has Texas-style cattle ranching east of the mountains, the Navajo Nation in the west, and the Mexican border to the south, Santa Fe is a southwestern microcosm.

Among Santa Fe's most noticeable characteristics is adobe-style architecture. The Spanish Pueblo Revival style, with protruding vigas (roof beams), is an adaptation of the Middle Eastern architecture brought to Spain by the Moors and to New Mexico by the Spanish, then influenced by Pueblo Indian construction techniques. The Territorial Revival style, with red bricks along the roofline, developed in the late 19th century with the introduction of building materials from the United States.

The city's Historic Styles Act, passed in 1957, requires that all new construction in the downtown historic district be Spanish Pueblo or Territorial in appearance, even though modern building methods and materials may be used. The law also limits building height and window space and prohibits large or electrified signs. The result, a low-rise, earth-tone city center preserving an Old World feel, is easy on the eyes.

Though museums and churches provide a framework for sightseeing, Santa Fe is a shopper's town, where Native American artifacts and traditional crafts, traditional western paintings, and contemporary Indian and non-Indian works of art, as well as aggressively regional Santa Fe-style "wearable art" fashions, are displayed in bewildering profusion. Quality is exceptional, with prices to match. Are you in the market for a painting that costs more than a car? If not, just browsing in the plaza area and Canyon Road galleries can introduce you to the visual glories of the American Southwest through the eyes of its best artists.

Note: The telephone area code for Albuquerque, Santa Fe, and Los Alamos is scheduled to change in 2002 to 557.

Suggested Schedule

9:00 a.m.	Drive the Turquoise Trail to Santa Fe.
10:30 a.m.	Stroll Santa Fe Plaza. See the Palace of the Governors, the New Mexico Fine Arts Museum, the IAIA Museum, and galleries.
1:00 p.m.	Green chile for lunch.
2:00 p.m.	Visit the Folk Art Museum or take an afternoon drive to Pecos.
Evening	Dinner and nightlife.

Travel Route: Albuquerque to Santa Fe (69 miles)

Drive the Turquoise Trail (NM 14) from Albuquerque to Santa Fe. It takes half an hour longer than I 25 North and is a calmer, prettier drive. From the "Big I" (where I 40 intersects I 25) in Albuquerque, take I 40 East 15 miles to exit 175 (Tijeras, Cedar Crest) and turn north (left) from the off-ramp.

The route takes you over the small but rugged Ortiz Range, site of the first gold discovery in what's now the United States. The former coal mining town of Madrid,

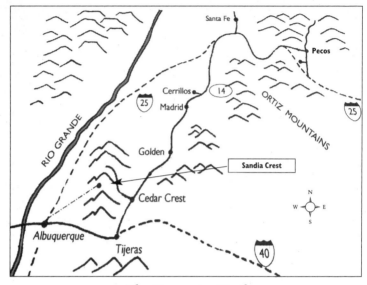

The Turquoise Trail

once nearly abandoned and now revived by artists and refugees from modern living, has a mining museum with an underground tour, as well as one of the Santa Fe area's livelier live music night spots, the Mine Shaft Tavern.

Cerrillos, an off-the-beaten-path village with few concessions to tourism (or to the 20th century) is worth a short stop and stroll. Follow the signs through town to the edge of the arroyo and visit Casa Grande, (505) 471-2744, an old 20-room adobe compound converted into a delightfully down-home bed and breakfast, petting zoo, and private museum of locally gathered turquoise, artifacts, and antique arroyo junk. If you have extra time, inquire at Casa Grande to arrange a personal four-wheel-drive and hiking tour of the old Pueblo Indian turquoise mines in the hills nearby.

If you have extra time to explore, detour south instead of north when you reach I 25 and visit El Rancho de las Golondrinas (exit 271 and follow the "Golondrinas Museum" signs). This well-preserved Spanish Colonial hacienda, circa 1710, was an important rest stop on the Camino Real from Mexico City. It is open for self-guided tours during the summer months—Wednesday through Sunday from 10:00 a.m. to 4:00 p.m.; adults $3.50, students 13 to 18 $2, children 5 to 12 $1. Several miles of walking trails afford tranquillity, and visitors are few except during Harvest Festival in early October, coinciding with the Kodak Albuquerque International Balloon Fiesta, when costumed volunteers re-create the colonial era.

When you reach I 25, don't continue into Santa Fe on NM 14 unless you're looking for a moderately priced motel. The highway becomes Cerrillos Road, a congested 6-mile strip that is Santa Fe's "other side of the tracks." Instead, take I 25 northbound for 6 miles to the Old Pecos Trail exit for a more attractive approach to downtown Santa Fe.

Downtown Walking Tour

One block east of the plaza or town square, on the north side of Palace Avenue, is Sena Plaza, a former Spanish colonial mansion whose interior courtyard provides a quiet, cool sitting spot. From there, proceed to the center of the plaza, where a monument commemorates Santa Feans' valor in repelling various 19th-century invaders such as Confederate troops and "_____ Indians." (The missing word, eradicated in broad daylight by an anonymous protester in the 1980s, was "savage." Locals hasten to point out that these weren't local Indians but rather Comanches who came from Texas—as, for that matter, did the Confederate soldiers.) Facing the plaza on the north side is the Palace of the Governors, housing the New Mexico Museum of History, a must-see for anyone interested in the region's Spanish colonial heritage. The next block west of the Palace is the New Mexico Fine Arts Museum. Allow at least two hours to see both museums. If you can't get enough of art museums, continue west on Palace Avenue, then go around the north side of the huge Eldorado Hotel; across the street you'll find the Georgia O'Keeffe Museum.

Returning from the art museums, walk diagonally across the plaza to La Fonda, Santa Fe's oldest hotel. Browse through the hotel's lobby, interesting for its unusual decor, then exit and continue west up San Francisco Street to St. Francis Cathedral. Across the street from the cathedral is the Institute of American Indian Arts Museum.

Leaving the IAIA Museum, return to La Fonda and turn left (south) down Old Santa Fe Trail one block to Loretto Chapel on the grounds of the Inn at Loretto. On the same street, across the river, is San Miguel Mission. Continue about two more blocks in the same direction on Old Santa Fe Trail to the New Mexico State Capitol Building, then backtrack to the plaza. At some point along this suggested tour, you'll probably be distracted by art galleries and shops. Wander and browse—you can't go wrong. Perhaps the one don't-miss-it among downtown galleries is the Gerald Peters Gallery, 1011 Paseo de Peralta, (505) 954-5700, the largest privately-owned art gallery in the United States, located a few blocks west of the plaza; walk beside the river on Alameda to get there.

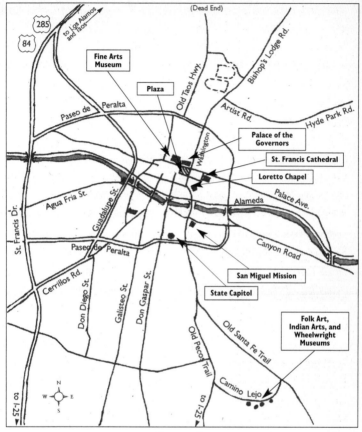

Santa Fe

Sightseeing Highlights

Palace of the Governors (New Mexico Museum of History)—
This is the oldest public building in the United States, dating
back to 1610. Emphasis is on the colonial and territorial
eras. Permanent exhibits include photographic reproduc-
tions of Spanish colonial maps of the Southwest as well as a

beautiful full-scale reconstruction of a Penitente chapel. Open daily from 10:00 a.m. to 5:00 p.m., closed Mondays off-season. Admission is $5 for adults, under 17 years old free; free to all on Friday evenings from 5:00 to 8:00 p.m. A multi-day pass for the Palace of the Governors, the Fine Arts Museum, the Museum of Indian Arts, and the Museum of International Folk Art costs $10 a person.

Indians selling jewelry and pottery at the Palace of the Governors portico enjoy official status as an "exhibit" of the Museum of New Mexico, which regulates the quality and authenticity of their goods.

New Mexico Fine Arts Museum—Built in 1917 to encourage Santa Fe's burgeoning artist colony, the museum with its stylized neo-Spanish Pueblo look sparked a resurgence of the architecture that characterizes Santa Fe today. The museum formerly provided display space for local artists as well as a framing workshop in the basement and free monthly banquets upstairs. In those days, Santa Fe's artist population was small enough to fit in one room. Today the upstairs galleries house classic paintings from early-20th-century Santa Fe and Taos. The main floor galleries rotate exhibits with emphasis on contemporary New Mexican artists. St. Francis Auditorium, adjoining the museum, is patterned after the interiors of early New Mexican mission churches, with a series of frescoes depicting Franciscan missionary history. The museum is open daily from 10:00 a.m. to 5:00 p.m., closed Mondays off-season. Admission $5 for adults, free under age 17.

Georgia O'Keeffe Museum—This privately endowed museum celebrates the work of New Mexico's most famous painter, who lived in Abiquiu and Santa Fe for more than 60 years before her death in 1986. The austere stucco museum galleries showcase rotating exhibits featuring many of O'Keeffe's best-known paintings as well as those of her contemporary modern artists. 135 Grant Street, (505) 946-1000. Open daily from 10:00 a.m. to 5:00 p.m., admission is $5 per person, free on Friday from 5:00 to 8:00 p.m.

IAIA Museum—Operated by the federal government, the Institute of American Indian Arts on Santa Fe's far southwest side provides free training for the most talented young Indian artists from all over the United States. Its presence has been a major factor in the emergence of Santa Fe as the largest market for contemporary Native American art. The institute's downtown museum, a converted former federal office building, houses the National Collection of Contemporary Indian Art and features changing special exhibitions, a performance gallery, and a museum shop. The museum is open daily from 9:00 a.m. (10:00 a.m. off-season) to 5:00 p.m. Admission is $4 for adults, $2 for senior citizens, students with I.D., and children under age 16; free on Friday from 5:00 to 8:00 p.m.

St. Francis Cathedral—This church was built in 1869 by Archbishop Jean Baptiste Lamy, the French clergyman who was transferred here from Cleveland, Ohio, to restore mainstream Catholicism to New Mexico. (The Mexican government had banished all Spanish-born priests 41 years before. In isolation from the mother church, spiritual needs were served by the Brothers of Light, a lay Penitente sect that remains alive and well in rural New Mexico. After U.S. occupation, both Catholic Church and the federal government feared the Brotherhood's influence.) The cathedral's most notable feature is La Conquistadora, housed to the left of the altar in a chapel that was part of the original church on this site. The blue-clad willow-wood statue of the Virgin, carried by Spanish refugees in their flight from the Pueblo Revolt of 1680, is the oldest surviving religious carving in New Mexico and the centerpiece of a thanksgiving procession (during Fiesta, the weekend after Labor Day) that has been held annually since 1716. Notice the inscription in Hebrew over the church doors; it was placed there as a symbol of unity between Santa Fe's Catholic and Jewish communities after the archbishop ran out of construction funds and a group of Jewish businessmen bailed him out, financing the completion of the roof, but not the planned Gothic towers, which remain truncated to this day.

Loretto Chapel (Chapel of Our Lady of Light)—Another Archbishop Lamy creation, the chapel is best known for its "miraculous staircase." Legend has it that the architect abandoned the project (some say he was caught with the bishop's nephew's wife) without building any stairs to the choir loft. A Mysterious Carpenter (the faithful believe he was St. Joseph, though skeptical historians claim he was an Austrian tourist) appeared and built this beautiful curved staircase without using any nails. Then he vanished without asking for payment. (Say, that *is* mysterious. . . .) Open daily from 8:00 a.m. to 6:00 p.m. in summer, 9:00 a.m. to 5:00 p.m. the rest of the year, admission $1.

San Miguel Mission—This chapel, claimed to be the oldest church in the United States, was built in 1710 on the rubble of a 1626 mission church destroyed during the Pueblo Revolt. Two other early mission churches still stand—at Ácoma (1629), which you may have visited on Day 6 or 7, and at Isleta (1630)—so whether this one really counts as the oldest church is a matter of controversy. It's old, though, and reveals the spiritual side of Spanish colonial life. Indian relics are on display from the centuries-old pueblo that was demolished to build the earlier church. Open Monday through Saturday from 9:00 a.m. to 4:30 p.m. and Sunday from 1:00 to 4:30 p.m. Donations are accepted. There is a Catholic curio shop.

State Capitol—A big circular flat-roofed neo-Territorial style building, the "Roundhouse" looks nothing like a capitol building is supposed to. Its floor plan was patterned after the Zia Pueblo sun symbol that graces the New Mexico flag and license plates. Stroll through the gardens, landscaped with vegetation from all parts of New Mexico, and the rotunda decorated with New Mexican art. A public gallery adjacent to the governor's office has changing regional art exhibits. A former state capitol, still the prettiest building in the state government complex, is the nearby Bataan Building, whose classic dome was removed in 1951. Open Monday through Friday from 8:00 a.m. to 5:00 p.m. and on Saturday during the summer months from 9:00 a.m. to 4:00 p.m.

Canyon Road—Drive up Canyon Road, the first left turn off Paseo de Peralta after you cross the river heading south, to see the original center of Santa Fe's artist colony, now a mixed bag of small studio/galleries and more commercial restaurants and shops. If Santa Fe's art scene has sparked an urge in you to take up sketching again (you'll find plenty of inspiration in the coming weeks), the Artisan on Canyon Road is among the most complete art supply stores you're ever likely to find.

Where Canyon Road stops being one-way, turn right on Camino del Monte Sol and drive south to Old Santa Fe

Trail. Take a one-block jog to your right (downhill) to Camino Lejo, with its big "Museums" sign, and turn there to find the following three museums where you can spend the whole morning and wish you had more time.

New Mexico Museum of Indian Arts and Culture— This outstanding museum presents selections from the state of New Mexico's 50,000 Indian artifacts, with Native American participation in exhibit planning, and works from the Institute of American Indian Art. One exhibit shows aerial photographs of Pueblo ruins that non-Indians cannot visit in person, including the ancient pueblo on Black Mesa above San Ildefonso Pueblo (Day 9). There are often craft demonstrations. The gift shop has an excellent selection of books on Indian subjects. Open daily from 10:00 a.m. to 5:00 p.m., closed Mondays off-season; admission $5 for adults, free under age 17.

New Mexico Museum of International Folk Art— Among the most unusual museums anywhere, this is the place in Santa Fe to take children if you have any along. It can also bring out the childlike wonder in you. Amble through the Spanish colonial and other folk art exhibits to the Girard Wing, where you'll find a phenomenal collection of handcrafted toys and miniatures from throughout the world arranged in enchanting dioramas. There are also temporary and permanent Hispanic heritage exhibits. Perhaps the most unique feature of this one-of-a-kind museum is an elevator that visitors can ride down to the basement to wander among drawers and shelves filled with thousands of folk art pieces that are not on display. The museum's gift shop is wonderful. Open daily from 10:00 a.m. to 5:00 p.m., closed Mondays off-season. Admission is $5 for adults, free under age 17.

Wheelwright Museum of American Indian Art—This small private museum features rotating traditional and modern Native American art exhibits. It was founded, with guidance from famed Navajo shaman Hosteen Klah, by Mary Wheelwright, daughter of an aristocratic Bostonian family who came west to live among the Indians. The building is in the eight-sided hogan shape that Navajo ceremonies require. Downstairs, Case Trading Post sells Native American arts and crafts of assured quality in all price ranges as well as books, posters, and handmade cards. Open Monday through Saturday from 10:00 a.m. to 5:00 p.m. and Sundays from 1:00 to 5:00 p.m. Suggested donation is $3 for adults, $2 for children under 12.

Randall Davey Audubon Center—If you'd rather be outdoors, make time in your morning schedule to visit the estate of a longtime Santa Fe artist who left his home and 135-acre grounds to the National Audubon Society as a wildlife refuge. At the mouth of Santa Fe Canyon (a municipal watershed that has been closed to the public for 50 years), wildlife that sometimes wanders down to these meadows includes coyotes, raccoons, black bears, mountain lions, bobcats, and mule deer. The refuge is home to over 100 species of birds and 120 species of plants. The grounds are open daily from 9:00 a.m. to 5:00 p.m. A $1 admission fee is requested from non-Audubon members. Call (505) 983-4609 for information on guided history tours of the Randall Davey house.

To get there, take Canyon Road as far as it goes. When it seems to end, jog one block to the right, then left onto Upper Canyon Road. The Randall Davey Center is as far up Upper Canyon Road as you're allowed to drive.

Lodging

Choosing to stay in town rather than camping tonight will give you a better chance to enjoy evening entertainment. Downtown hotels are luxurious and costly.

My favorite Santa Fe luxury lodgings are at **Hotel Santa Fe,** 1501 Paseo de Peralta at Cerrillos Road, (505) 982-1200 or (800) 825-9876. This exceptionally comfortable Pueblo Revival–style hotel, decorated with Native American art including numerous bronze works by famed Apache sculptor Allan Houser, is unique in that it is 51 percent owned by an Indian pueblo. The federal government makes economic development funds available to Indian tribes under the Indian Financing Act of 1974, and these funds are usually used to start businesses—from bingo parlors to chopstick factories—on the reservations. But tiny Picurís Pueblo, hidden deep in the Sangre de Cristo Mountains, opted to invest its government funding in Santa Fe tourism. The hotel provides employment and the main source of income for the pueblo. It's about eight blocks from the plaza, and a free shuttle runs between the hotel and downtown every half hour. Rates start at $149 during the summer season, as low as $119 off-season.

Among the numerous other luxury hotels within walking distance of the plaza are **La Fonda,** $200 and up, 100 E. San Francisco Street, (505) 982-5511, Santa Fe's oldest hotel and still one of the best; and the Victorian-style **Hotel St. Francis,** 210 Don Gaspar Street, $100 and up, (505) 983-5700.

Santa Fe has several bed-and-breakfast inns. Since a city ordinance restricts B&Bs to areas with commercial zoning, most are within easy walking distance of the plaza. Check out the **Grant Corner Inn,** 122 Grant Street, (505) 983-6678, a turn-of-the-century brick mansion in a prime location a block west and a block north of the Fine Arts Museum, where rates range from $90 up, full breakfast included.

You'll find several lower-cost motels along busy Cerrillos Road, which runs for miles diagonally southwest from downtown. The best rates close to downtown are at the **Santa Fe Plaza Travelodge,** 646 Cerrillos Road, (505) 982-3551, where doubles start at $60, and the **Santa Fe Motel,** 510 Cerrillos Road, (505) 982-1039, starting at $90 in season and $60 off-season.

Warning: Santa Fe accommodations tend to fill up quickly on Wednesday through Saturday nights during Opera season, mid-July through mid-August, so if you are traveling without reservations, check into your hotel or motel as soon as you arrive in town, before sightseeing or eating. Another warning: For Indian Market weekend, the third weekend in August, all accommodations in the Santa Fe area are booked up as much as four months in advance, and it may be impossible to find lodging on short notice even in Albuquerque or Los Alamos!

Food

Green chile is what distinguishes New Mexican cuisine from any other. New Mexicans grow more chile peppers than the rest of the United States combined and prefer to eat them as a roasted, peeled, and usually diced vegetable, by the bowlful or poured over practically anything. The quality of chile is judged by how "hot" it is, so restaurants compete to bring tears of ecstasy to their patrons' eyes.

When a waitress asks, "Red or green?" don't make the common error of assuming that green must be milder than red. The green chile at any self-respecting Santa Fe restaurant will knock your socks off.

For regional cuisine in Santa Fe, there are myriad possibilities. Downtown, **The Shed**, 133½ East Palace Avenue, (505) 982-9030, is a visitors' favorite in a historic Territorial-style building with an atmospheric courtyard. **Tia Sophia's**, 210 West San Francisco Street, (505) 983-9880, is an unpretentious coffee shop for breakfast or lunch. The spicy food here is guaranteed to wake you up! A few blocks west of downtown in the railroad yards, **Tomasita's**, 500 South Guadalupe Street, (505) 983-5721, is probably the best-known New Mexican restaurant, with muy picante lunches and dinners, including daily specials, at moderate prices.

When it comes to authentic New Mexican food, locals prefer restaurants away from the plaza, such as **La Choza**, located near the intersection of St. Francis Drive and Cerrillos Road at 905 Alarid Street, (505) 982-0909. ("La choza" means "the shed" in Spanish, and this intimate little restaurant is run by the same family as The Shed downtown.) Another local favorite is **Maria's New Mexican Kitchen**, located just east of St. Francis Drive at 555 West Cordova Road, (505) 983-7929.

The **Corn Dance Cafe**, 1500 Paseo de Peralta, (505) 982-1200, in the lobby of the Hotel Santa Fe, is Santa Fe's only American Indian restaurant. It features a full range of native foods of North America—Maya-style mango-and-jicama salad, Potawatomi prairie chicken, "kick-ass" buffalo chili, Tlingit alder-smoked salmon, and many other choices.

Mexican cuisine, distinctively different from New Mexican food, is also well-represented in Santa Fe. Best in town, most locals would agree, is **Los Mayas,** just west of downtown off Guadalupe Street at 409 West Water Street, (505) 986-9930; the menu features such specialties as plantain tamales in *mole poblano* sauce. Another local favorite, **Mariscos La Playa,** features Mexican-style seafood specialties, including fresh fish or shrimp ceviche tostadas; there are two locations—537 West Cordova Road, (505) 982-2790, and 2875 Cerrillos Road, (505) 473-4594.

Santa Fe has about 200 restaurants, constantly changing, serving everything from Greek grape leaves to green chile tempura. Survival, especially for restaurants located away from downtown, depends on keeping a local clientele during the long winter off-season. Most Santa Feans would agree that the best not-necessarily-New Mexican food in town is found not at pricey downtown glamor spots like the Coyote Cafe or the Old House, but at the unpretentious **Harry's Roadhouse,** (505) 989-4629, located slightly out of town on Old Las Vegas Highway, which parallels Interstate 25 east of the Old Pecos Trail freeway exit. Master chef Harry Shapiro's labor of love, the roadhouse has indoor and outdoor seating in summer and features entrees that range from turkey and green chile meat loaf to Morroccan couscous with squash and chickpeas, as well as daily seafood specials and imaginative one-time-only creations.

When stocking up on picnic supplies, be sure to pick up a loaf or two of the delicious homemade bread, baked in horno ovens, that Indian vendors sell on the streets around the plaza. The only way to take green chile back home is in the form of jelly, jam, or relish, available in many gift shops. Other great edible souvenirs are piñon nuts, red chile *ristras,* and Indian blue corn. Blue corn tortilla chips are sold in Santa Fe supermarkets. Blue cornmeal can be boiled into a tasty hot cereal called *atole,* similar to Cream of Wheat, or substituted in any recipe that uses cornmeal (use buttermilk instead of regular milk for a brighter blue color). Pueblo Indians, who hold blue corn sacred, make it into a crisp paper-thin bread called *piki* for festivals and religious ceremonies.

Camping

A good camping area near Santa Fe is the National Forest **Black Canyon Campground** or adjoining **Hyde Memorial State Park,** both 7 miles up Hyde Park–Ski Basin Road from downtown (take Washington Street north from downtown and turn right at the sign). Overnight parking (no hookups, no tent sites) is also allowed 10 miles farther up the road at the Ski Basin parking area, a major Pecos Wilderness trailhead with picnic tables and rest rooms.

Hyde Park is nearly 9,000 feet in altitude, compared with 5,000 feet in Albuquerque and 7,000 feet in Santa Fe. The Ski Basin parking lot is over 10,000 feet, about the same as the summit of Sandia Crest. Higher elevations mean cooler temperatures. Each 1,000 feet of altitude drops the temperature about 9 degrees, as great a difference as traveling 300 miles north, so temperatures at Hyde Park average 35 degrees cooler than in Albuquerque, about the same as in Calgary, Alberta. Nights can be chilly at any time of year. In early October the road from Hyde Park to the Ski Basin becomes a "must-see" sight, as autumn colors brighten the largest continuous forest of aspen trees in the world.

Hiking and Biking

The short, strenuous **Atalaya Trail** starts at St. John's College on Camino Cruz Blanca, a short distance east of the Folk Art and Indian Arts museums. It climbs two miles with a 2,000-foot elevation gain to the summit of Atalaya Mountain, offering higher and higher panoramic views of the city.

Also close to the east edge of the city are 22 miles of mostly easy, year-round hiking trails in the **Dale Ball Foothills Trail System,** newly opened in 2001. Look for the parking area and map of the complex hiking-and-biking trail network along Hyde Park Road at the junction with Sierra del Norte Road.

For hiking at higher altitudes, take Hyde Park/Ski Basin Road into the mountains east of town. There are several trailheads along the way. The end of the 17-mile paved road, a ski area in winter, is also the most-used trailhead into the **Pecos Wilderness,** with its boundless wilderness trail network. (Careful—the Ski Basin trailhead is 10,500 feet above sea level. If sea level is where you come from, the thin atmosphere may restrict strenuous exercise.)

The vehicles-prohibited maintenance road that runs six miles up to the 12,010-foot summit of Lake Peak from the **Aspen Vista** parking area midway between Hyde Park and the Ski Basin is a wonderful mountain bike route.

Nightlife

From the moment you leave Santa Fe until you reach Las Vegas two weeks from now, evening entertainment will consist of crackling campfires, spectacularly starry skies, and an occasional ranger slide show. If you want to get out and boogie, tonight's the night.

The larger downtown hotels all have lounges, piano bars, or the like. For quiet, cozy elegance, stop in at the **Staab House** bar in La Posada, 330 East Palace Avenue, (505) 986-0000, with its authentic Victorian-era furnishings and notorious resident ghost. Ask anyone who works there about her.

If country dancing is your passion, set those achy, breaky feet in motion at **Rodeo Nites**, 2911 Cerrillos Road, (505) 473-4138, presenting live C&W bands nightly.

A good place to meet Santa Fe locals is **El Farol** on Canyon Road at Palace Avenue (505) 983-9912, a friendly neighborhood bar in an uncommon neighborhood. Folk musicians perform some nights for a small cover. There are rarely any open tables after 9:00 p.m. Join a group of strangers and you'll find yourself welcome. It's that kind of place.

Santa Fe's summer calendar is packed with cultural performances and spectator events. The most famous is the **Santa Fe Opera**, 3 miles north of town on US 285, mid-July through mid-August. Tickets are expensive and hard to get on short notice, but if you dress as elegantly as possible (wearing blue jeans to the opera is considered déclassé, though many locals used to and some still do) and ask at the box office, your chances of getting inexpensive standing-room tickets are good. Call (505) 982-3855 for information.

For something completely different in the way of theater entertainment, consider the **Madrid Melodrama**, held during the summer months in the town of Madrid, which you went through on the Turquoise Trail this morning. Melodramas for tourists can be found throughout the west in the summer, but this one is the most authentic I've ever witnessed, with its straight-faced presentations of genuine Victorian plays in an old railroad barn that recalls the kinds of places where touring companies actually performed in small towns a century ago. The playhouse even has a real locomotive, adding realism when the script calls for a heroine to be tied to the railroad tracks. Bring a bag of marshmallows and learn firsthand why they came to be known as "villain bullets." Tickets cost $10. Call (505) 473-0743 for current performance information.

Other events range from the **Santa Fe Chamber Music Festival** to the **Rodeo de Santa Fe.** Check the weekly (Thursday to Wednesday) *Reporter* or the *Santa Fe New Mexican*'s Friday "Pasatiempo" supplement for complete entertainment listings and reviews.

Many Santa Fe visitors have told me that their most memorable experience was a starlight hot tub soak at **Ten Thousand Waves,** a Japanese-style spa on Hyde Park Road near the national forest boundary. Pricey but well worth it. (505) 992-5025.

Ten miles north of Santa Fe on US 285, Tesuque Pueblo's **Camel Rock Casino,** (505) 984-8414, offers not only the usual fun and games but also a full schedule of concerts that tend to feature blasts from the past. Recent acts have included the Moody Blues, Glen Campbell, and Blue Oyster Cult.

Bookstores

Residents of the "City Different" are fiercely loyal to established local independent bookstores in the face of mounting chain competition. You'll find readings and author appearances almost daily. Here are some of the top contenders:

Collected Works, 208-B West San Francisco, (505) 988-4226.

Garcia Street Books, 376 Garcia Street, (505) 986-0151.

The Ark, 133 Romero Street, (505) 988-3709.

Good Books, 526 West Cordova Road, (505) 992-1900.

The Travel Bug, Montezuma and Guadalupe Streets, (505) 992-0418.

Itinerary Option: Pecos

For a pleasant afternoon outdoors, drive about 20 miles east (northbound) from Santa Fe on I 25 to the second Pecos exit and visit Pecos National Historical Park, the site of a major pueblo ruin that dates back to the 13th century and a Spanish mission from the 17th century. The Pecos pueblo was the eastern gateway to the Rio Grande pueblo country, and it prospered through trade. A long, massive wall, still partly standing, separated the pueblo from the camping area for visiting groups of Indians from the eastern plains. The pueblo was abandoned in the mid-1800s after Comanche raids wiped out much of the population, and the survivors' descendants now live at Jemez Pueblo in the mountains north of Albuquerque. Open daily from 8:00 a.m. to 5:00 p.m. during the summer months, until 5:00 p.m. the rest of the year. Admission is $4 per vehicle.

In the 1980s, the park used to be just 365 acres in size. In response to citizen concerns about large-scale real estate development in the area, the U.S. government authorized acquisition of the adjoining 5,500-acre ranch owned by actress Greer Garson. It also added two tracts of land nearby where the westernmost battle of the Civil War took place and changed the monument to a national historical park. The additional land includes a beautiful 2-mile stretch of the Pecos River well removed from the highway. Access is restricted, since the government has never been able to work out a satisfactory agreement with the nearby village of Pecos to accommodate a flood of park visitors.

After visiting the park, you may wish to continue west through the village and enjoy a scenic 20-mile drive up the Pecos River Canyon, a popular trout-fishing area with enclaves of vacation cabins. The pavement ends at the Terrero General Store, and from there an unpaved road that can be quite rough and hard on vehicles leads to a series of free campgrounds and trailheads at the edge of the Pecos Wilderness. Midway up the paved portion of the road, a dirt road turns off into Dalton Canyon, used as a hideout by the notorious outlaw Dalton Gang for many years in the late 19th century. The canyon is a pretty spot for walking and picnicking.

Bandelier National Monument and Los Alamos

Los Alamos, White Rock, and Bandelier National Monument occupy parts of the Pajarito Plateau, a ledge of lava and ash formed by a huge volcano. If you could view the area from above, you would see that the mountain range to the west is actually circular, the crumbled remains of the rim of the volcano, which some geologists believe stood higher than Mount Everest some 1,700,000 years ago.

The plateau and volcano caldera have been nominated for national park status three times—first in 1919 and most recently in 1986. Certainly, the area's scenic beauty and unique features rival those of the Grand Canyon, Yosemite, or Yellowstone. All three attempts were blocked by ranching and forest products interests, but in 1998 the U.S. Congress resumed negotiations to buy the privately-owned ranchland in the crater of the volcano. When opened for public recreation in 2002, this land along with adjacent Hells Canyon Recreation Area, Bandelier National Monument, and parts of Santa Fe National Forest will encompass all of the area originally proposed for national park status—except for the land now occupied by the town of Los Alamos or controlled by Los Alamos National Laboratories. Side by side along the base of the ancient volcano, you'll find pre-Columbian Indian ruins, present-day Indian pueblos, and the birthplace of the nuclear age.

The area is a one-hour drive from Santa Fe. Along the way you can visit Indian pueblos and an outdoor sculpture gallery.

Note: The telephone area code for Albuquerque, Santa Fe, and Los Alamos is scheduled to change in 2002 to 557.

Suggested Schedule

8:00 a.m.	Breakfast in Santa Fe.
9:00 a.m.	Drive to Bandelier National Monument, visiting Shidoni's sculpture gardens and San Ildefonso Pueblo en route.
11:30 a.m.	Arrive at Bandelier. Explore the Indian ruins and enjoy a picnic lunch.
2:00 p.m.	Stay in Bandelier for an afternoon of hiking or explore the Los Alamos area.
5:00 p.m.	Take your choice: return to Santa Fe, camp at Bandelier, or spend the night in Los Alamos or White Rock.

Travel Route: Santa Fe to Bandelier and Los Alamos (40 miles)

Washington Street in downtown Santa Fe becomes Bishop's Lodge Road as it crosses Paseo de Peralta heading north. Follow this winding, hilly road through Tesuque, a pricey rural suburb of Santa Fe, where resident celebrities like Oprah Winfrey, Val Kilmer, and Ali

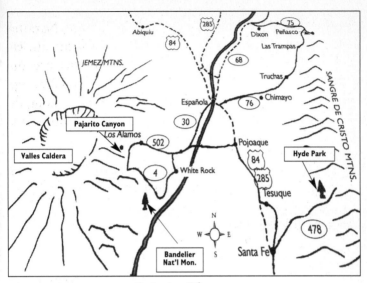

Pajarito Plateau

McGraw own homes. Watch for Shidoni Art Foundry on your left and stop in to walk around acres of parklike outdoor sculpture gallery. If you own a skyscraper or shopping mall and want a really large piece of art to put in front of it, here's where you can buy one.

Continuing past the intersection at Tesuque Village Market, the local grocery store, café, and gourmet deli, the road eventually joins four-lane US 84/285. Follow the main highway north for 9 miles to Pojoaque, where a freeway-style exit ramp puts you on NM 502 heading west to Los Alamos and Bandelier.

After about 5 miles, you'll see the turnoff on your right to San Ildefonso Pueblo. In another 3 miles, you'll cross the Rio Grande. (Bandelier National Monument, your destination, is just 17 miles from Santa Fe as the crow flies, but you have to drive more than twice that distance because this is the only bridge over the river.) The road divides 4 miles past the river, one fork going to Los Alamos and the other to White Rock, where you may wish to make a short detour to White Rock Canyon Overlook before continuing on your way to Bandelier National Monument.

Leaving Bandelier, if you turn left from the entrance instead of backtracking to the right, you will reach a short-cut to Los Alamos in a few miles. (If you stay on the main road, you will climb steeply to the rim of Valle Grande.) The Los Alamos turnoff takes you past hidden Pajarito Canyon. When you pass the Los Alamos National Laboratories administration complex, turn left at the stoplight, cross the bridge that spans Los Alamos Canyon, and then turn right on Trinity Drive to reach the Los Alamos business district. Jog one block north at the first opportunity to reach the Los Alamos County Historical Museum and Fuller Lodge Art Gallery.

Leaving Los Alamos, Trinity Drive will put you back on NM 502 for a spectacular, edgy descent along colorful canyon walls. If driving spectacular, edgy roads makes you uncomfortable, you can avoid this one by backtracking the way you came.

Sightseeing Highlights

Pojoaque—Although it is the tribal headquarters of the Pojoaque Indian Reservation, no trace remains of the ancestral pueblo. After a smallpox epidemic nearly wiped out all but two dozen members of the tribe in the 1920s, the old pueblo fell into disrepair and was eventually demolished to make way for a roadside shopping strip and the trailer park where many of the Pojoaque people live today. The tribe's fortunes improved in 1993, when they converted their old high school into the Cities of Gold Casino, one of several Indian gaming palaces along the main highway between Santa Fe and Taos (open 24 hours; 505-455-3313).

Aside from the casino, Pojoaque's main visitor attraction is the Poeh Center (505-455-3460), an Indian cultural center jointly operated by the Eight Northern Pueblos (Tesuque, Nambé, Pojoaque, San Ildefonso, Santa Clara, San Juan, Picuris, and Taos). The center includes a museum of Pueblo art and artifacts, as well as a large gift shop. A full-size replica of part of the ancestral pueblo stands behind the center and forms a backdrop for ceremonial dances held at Pojoaque on feast days.

San Ildefonso Pueblo—While the most striking Indian pueblos in New Mexico—Taos and Acoma—seem like fragments of the ancient past, San Ildefonso typifies the blend of traditional and contemporary ways of life found in most pueblos along the Rio Grande. The central plaza is much larger than those at most other pueblos; unlike the others, San Ildefonso has two separage kiva clans, so during ceremonies two dances are often held simultaneously on opposite sides of the plaza. The mission-style church was built around 1970 to replace an old one. Behind the pueblo rises a massive volcanic rock formation called Black Mesa. A sacred spot to the San Ildefonso people, whose ancestors retreated to live on top of it when the Spanish returned after the Pueblo Revolt of 1680, the mesa is forbidden to non-Indians.

Traditional arts and crafts are an important part of life at San Ildefonso Pueblo. The distinctive, raku-like black pottery style developed at San Ildefonso by the late Maria

Martinez (a video about her is shown at national parks and monuments throughout the Four Corners area) is prized by collectors and found in museums around the world. A collection of Maria's pottery can be seen upon request at the Popovi Da Studio in the pueblo, open daily during the summer months from 10:00 a.m. to 5:00 p.m., closed weekends and Wednesday during May and October. The pueblo also has a small museum, open during the summer on weekdays only from 8:00 a.m. to 5:00 p.m.

Visitors who wish to walk around the pueblo must check in at the tribal administration office first. The main reason for this is to make sure you know about the pueblo's rule prohibiting photography, which is strictly enforced and can result in confiscation of violators' cameras.

Bandelier National Monument—The birthplace of Southwestern archaeology, now a hikers' paradise, is named for Adolph Bandelier, a Swiss immigrant and self-taught Native American scholar. In 1880, he was the first archaeologist to excavate and study Indian ruins instead of looting them for collectible artifacts. Unexcavated pueblo ruins, found throughout the Jemez Mountains, are crumbled, buried, hard to recognize, and not much to look at. (See for yourself by making a stop at Tsankawi, an unrestored ruin in a separate unit of Bandelier National Monument on the way to White Rock. It has ancient foot trails, rock art, and a fabulous view, but the large old pueblo site is only barely discernable.) Bandelier's excavation was the prototype for restoring all the ancient pueblo ruins that are visitor attractions today. His philosophy of restoring ruins so that non-scientists could appreciate them soon spread to other parts of the world. Sylvanus Morley, who met Bandelier while he was a professor at Santa Fe's School of American Archaeology, subsequently devoted his life to the restoration of Chichén Itzá in the Yucatán, one of the most ambitious archaeological projects ever undertaken and today Mexico's most popular tourist attraction.

The ruins behind the WPA-era stone visitors center stand as the crowning achievement of Bandelier's 34 years of work. The settlement dates from the Postclassic Pueblo period—around 1400, which followed the abandonment of Mesa Verde and Chaco Canyon, covered elsewhere in this book. The inhabitants are believed to have been the ancestors of the San Ildefonso Pueblo people.

Only a stone floor plan remains of what was once a three-story castlelike walled town, now called Frijoles Pueblo because it is in Frijoles Canyon, so called because Spanish explorers found wild remnants of ancient bean fields there. Nearby cliff dwellings are better preserved. Climb the wooden ladders to the Ceremonial Cave for the best view of the ruins and their magnificent setting.

The road takes you in only to the corner of the monument. Beyond the visitors center and ruins, 70 miles of foot trails offer access to a rugged 32,000-acre hikers-only wilderness area. Admission to the national monument is $10 per vehicle. Dogs and other pets are prohibited on backcountry hiking trails.

Los Alamos—The hidden site of the ultimate Top Secret Government Project during World War II is now a cozy all-American community with incomparable views. It's a company town for Los Alamos National Laboratories, so big you can't miss it. (You can't go in, either, without a security clearance.) Following the end of the Cold War, the existence of the lab—and thus the town—was threatened by massive budget cuts until 1999, when Los Alamos became the epicenter of a spy scandal that convinced some law-makers of the need for continued nuclear weapons research and development.

To learn more about the development of nuclear weapons—as well as other programs like solar and geo-thermal energy and genetic mapping that LANL scientists could be working on if they weren't so busy building bombs—visit the **Bradbury Science Museum**, where you'll see mementos of the Manhattan Project, hands-on com-puter and laser exhibits, an antique atomic bomb, and explanations of other technologies developed at the lab which are difficult to pronounce, let alone comprehend. The museum is open Tuesday through Friday from 9:00 a.m. to 5:00 p.m., Saturday through Monday 1:00 to 5:00 p.m. Central Avenue and 15th Street; 505-667-4444. Admission is free.

The **Los Alamos County Historical Museum** and **Fuller Lodge Art Center** occupy buildings of the pre-World War II Los Alamos Ranch School, where children from wealthy eastern families were sent to get healthy through outdoor living. The historical museum tells about the joys and rigors of life at the ranch school, as well as the war years at Los Alamos. Fuller Lodge Art Center pro-vides exhibition space for a community cooperative of local artists, a refreshing contrast to Santa Fe's big-money art market. Near the corner of Central Avenue and 20th Street, the historical museum (505-662-9331) is open Monday through Saturday from 10:00 a.m. to 4:00 p.m., and the art museum (505-662-6272) Monday through Saturday from 9:30 a.m. to 4:30 p.m., Sundays from 11:00 a.m. to 5:00 p.m. There is a small pueblo ruin in the park behind the lodge. Admission is free; donations are welcome.

Visitors to Los Alamos will also see the scars of the forest fire that started as a prescribed burn in nearby Bandelier National Monument, ran out of control and swept across about one-quarter of Los Alamos, forcing the evacuation of 26,000 people and leaving more than 300 families homeless.

White Rock Canyon Overlook—As you drive into the Los Alamos bedroom community of White Rock on your way to Bandelier National Monument, turn left on Rover Drive and follow the signs to the overlook, located in a municipal park on the tip of the mesa. Seven hundred feet below runs a wild stretch of the Rio Grande. To the north, Black Mesa looms at the end of the canyon, and beyond it you can see the rugged Sangre de Cristo Mountains running all the way up into Colorado. Behind you, a thin waterfall plunges into a side canyon. The river below can be reached by any of three rugged trails that descend to the canyon bottom in less than a mile. You can see one of the trails toward your right from the overlook, but finding its starting point is trickier. The trailhead, well hidden near the picnic area about a hundred yards to the right of the overlook, is marked only by two old fence posts on the rim.

Cliff Dwellings—There are over 10,000 known archaeological sites on the Pajarito Plateau. In fact, around 1400, more people lived in this area than are here today. If you look closely, you can see the remnants of cliff dwellings on the south-facing side of every canyon, most easily spotted by the manmade holes that once held roof supports. For a closer look, obtain a Santa Fe National Forest map from any Santa Fe sporting goods store and check out one of the unpaved roads that run up hidden canyons, such as Garcia

Canyon. Many of these cliff dwelling sites are littered with pottery shards and other artifacts. Remember, not only is it illegal to remove these, but many locals will confirm that those who take pottery shards will be plagued by a curse—the last thing you need on a driving vacation—which can only be broken by returning them. (Speaking of curses, a word of caution: If a locked gate or no-trespassing sign indicates that an area is off-limits, *keep out!* Back in the 1940s they were very casual about disposing of nuclear waste, and they also planted land mines that were never removed, so a few areas around Los Alamos are permanently radioactive or explosive.)

Pajarito Canyon—Follow NM 501, the paved road that goes west (uphill, toward the mountains) from the stoplight near the LANL administration complex. The road curves around to the south amd passes a paved side road on the right that goes to the Los Alamos Ski Area. Continue past the turnoff for about half a mile and watch for the next road on the right, an unpaved, unmarked forest road and informal picnic area that runs in both directions parallel to the main road. Park beside this road and walk the dirt road north (downhill); it curves to the west, following a small creek, and ends after a quarter of a mile, but a foot trail continues up Pajarito Canyon from here. What distinguishes this from the other dozen or so canyons in the area is the narrow passageway betweeen sheer rock walls which prevented the removal of timber from the canyon. This is one of the few areas of untouched ancient forest in the Jemez Mountains, lush and magnificent. Locals refer to it as "the rain forest." Black bears are sometimes spotted in the canyon.

Valles Caldera National Preserve—Continuing on NM 503 west beyond the Bandelier National Monument entrance for about 10 steep miles, you will reach the upper rim of the Jemez Mountains and soon see Valles Caldera, which is said to be the world's largest volcano caldera, covering 175 square miles with a smaller, more recent volcano cone in its center. It would look very much like Crater Lake in Oregon, except that a narrow canyon on the far side lets the water run out. Is the volcano extinct? Consider the fact that dozens of hot springs exist throughout the area. On the west side of the caldera, Los Alamos National Laboratories maintains a geothermal pilot project to experiment with ways to convert the earth's heat to useful energy. Something is causing all that heat so close beneath the surface. Extinct? Don't bet on it!

This area was acquired by the federal government in August 2000 and is expected to be opened for public recreation by August 2002. It is home to one of the largest elk herds in the United States.

Food

Although fast food chains dominate the restaurant scene in Los Alamos and White Rock, there are several good, family-run places that serve Mexican and New Mexican food. The longest-established of these is **De Colores**, 820 Trinity Drive, (505) 662-6285. Top of the line is **Salsa's Gourmet Mexican**, 3801 Arkansas Avenue, (505) 662-2344. Other spicy choices include **Chili Works**, 1743 Trinity Drive, (505) 662-2005; and **Montoya's**, 813 Central Avenue, (505) 662-7026.

Los Alamos has a plentitude of Chinese restaurants—as

many, in fact, as the much larger city of Santa Fe. The following are all good, featuring consistently fresh ingredients and subtle spices: the **Hunan Garden Chinese Restaurant**, 1400 17th Street, (505) 662-0411; **Twin Dragon City**, 1377 Diamond Drive, (505) 662-5439; **Szechwan Chinese Restaurant**, 1504 Iris Street, (505) 662-3180; the **China Palace Restaurant**, 759 Central Avenue, (505) 662-4433; and, in White Rock, the **Chinshan Inn**, 124 Longview Drive, (505) 672-1433.

Many Los Alamos restaurants do not serve breakfast or lunch on weekends.

Lodging

You won't find an abundance of accommodations in this area because most travelers visit Bandelier National Monument and Los Alamos as a day trip from Santa Fe. While Los Alamos has only two motels—the **Los Alamos Inn,** 2201 Trinity Drive, (505) 662-7211, and the **Best Western Hilltop House Hotel**, 400 Trinity Drive, (505) 662-2441—about a dozen small bed and breakfasts have sprung up in the residential section of town. Try the **Adobe Pines Bed & Breakfast,** a contemporary Southwestern-style home overlooking the municipal golf course, 2101 Loma Linda Drive, (505) 662-6761; the **North Road Inn**, 2127 North Road, (505) 662-3678; or **Renatta's Orange Street Bed & Breakfast**, 3496 Orange Street, (505) 662-2651.

Another lodging possibility in the area is the new Indian-owned **Cities of Gold Hotel,** across the parking lot from the casino of the same name in Pojoque, US 84/285, (505) 455-0515. Rates are reasonable and the rooms are comfortably spacious. The location leaves something to be desired, though anyone who wants to stay within five minutes' walk of slot machines and a liquor store will find it ideal.

Camping

Bandelier National Monument has a campground on top of the mesa with an easy walking trail to the canyon rim for evening walks. There are nightly campfire talks and running water, but no hookups. Camping costs $10 plus park admission.

The only other campground in the area is a free municipal camping area 1 mile east of Los Alamos, besides the highway just before the beginning of the canyon descent. The campground is completely paved and has all the charm of a supermarket parking lot, but the view is breathtaking. There's a dumping station.

Hiking and Biking

A round-trip hike to the far boundary would take three full days. For an enjoyable day hike, explore more of Frijoles Canyon. The **Falls Trail**, downstream from the end of the backpackers' parking area across the bridge from the visitors center, is a 1½-mile (one-way) hike that packs cool creekside forests, cliffs, volcanic tent rocks, and a lovely waterfall view into a challenging 2½-hour hike. For a longer all-afternoon or even all-day excursion, get a free wilderness permit from the visitors center and hike the **Upper Frijoles Trail**, rockhopping and sometimes splashing back and forth across the creek. Watch for golden eagles, turkey vultures, and red-tailed hawks overhead. Go as far as you like; the trail continues about 8 miles to the upper end of the canyon. (This is a more enjoyable day hike than the more popular **Stone Lions Trail**, a hot, dry trip that's much more strenuous than it appears on the map because midway it traverses Alamo Canyon, both deeper and steeper than Frijoles Canyon.)

Bookstores

Los Alamos residents tend to be highly educated, and although most people here shop in Santa Fe, there are a technical and computer bookstore with coffee bar, a science bookstore next to the Bradbury Science Museum, and a good selection of local and regional books in the Los Alamos Historical Museum.

R Books, 111 Central Park Square, (505) 662-7257.

Otowi Station Bookstore, 1350 Central Avenue, (505) 662-9589.

Los Alamos Historical Museum Shop, 1921 Juniper, (505) 662-4493.

Taos

The High Road to Taos takes you through old Spanish colonial villages and into Carson National Forest, then descends to Rio Grande State Park. In the Taos area, visit Taos Pueblo and perhaps D. H. Lawrence's ranch.

The northernmost outpost of Spanish colonial America, founded five years after Santa Fe, Taos was the third permanent European settlement in what's now the United States. It was a major center for trade with people who weren't allowed farther into Spanish territory—the Navajo, Ute, and plains tribes as well as French and Anglo mountain men.

In 1898, two American artists, Bert Phillips and Ernest Blumenschein, were bound for Mexico on a sketching expedition but made it only as far as Taos before their wagon broke down. Enchanted by the land, the exotic people, and the strangely vivid quality of the light, they stayed to form the nucleus of Taos' active artist community. Other artists came to Taos from Europe at the outbreak of World War I, and beginning in the 1920s the town's cultural scene enjoyed international renown as the "Left Bank" of the American frontier.

The economy of Taos depends almost entirely on tourism, skiing, and the arts (perhaps a continuation of its historic role—trading with "barbarians" from the north). With its beautiful setting and rich tricultural heritage, it may be among the best places in the world to live if you don't need a job. The largest employer in Taos County is the Highway Department.

Suggested Schedule

8:00 a.m.	Breakfast.
9:00 a.m.	Drive the High Road to Taos, visiting old Spanish villages en route.
Noon	Arrive in Taos. Stroll the Plaza and Kit Carson Park.
1:30 p.m.	Visit Taos Pueblo
3:30 p.m.	Visit Martinez Hacienda, Kit Carson Home and Blumenschein Home.
6:00 p.m.	Dinner. Spend the night in Taos.

Travel Route: Los Alamos to Taos (80 miles)

From Los Alamos, White Rock, or Bandelier, descend the Pajarito Plateau on NM 502 and, before reaching the Rio Grande, turn left on the paved back road to Española, which parallels the river and takes you past Black Mesa and Santa Clara Pueblo. The road to Puye Cliff Dwellings turns off to the west midway along this road. The cliff dwellings, the ancestral home of the Santa Clara people since the 12th century, extend in several levels for about 2 miles along the face of the cliff. You can see the cliff dwellings at a distance before deciding whether to pay the $5-per-person (students and seniors $4) admission charge,

144

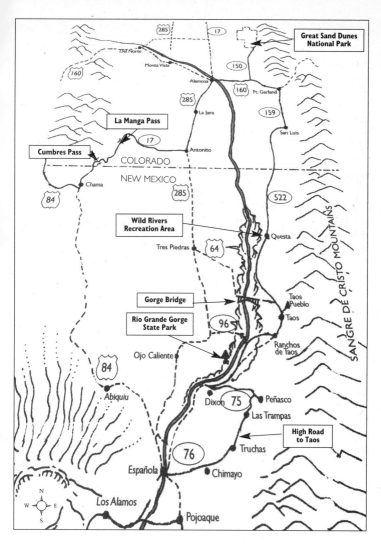

Upper Rio Grande Valley

which goes to Santa Clara Pueblo. There is also a large pueblo ruin on top of the mesa, partially restored and still used for ceremonies by residents of the modern pueblo.

From Española, turn right and drive through town to find NM 76 east to Chimayo, 10 miles into the foothills of the Sangre de Cristo range. As you approach Chimayo, watch for the sign to Santuario and follow it. Santuario de Chimayo, a small twin-towered church built entirely without nails in 1816, is believed by northern New Mexico's Catholics to be a place of miracles—the Lourdes of the American frontier. In a small room through another room to the left of the altar is El Pozito ("the little well"), where for over two centuries the faithful have taken pinches of clay for its healing properties. The crutches and braces in the adjoining room have been left as testimony that it works. Between Good Friday and Easter, thousands of people from throughout northern New Mexico line the roads, some carrying crosses, in pilgrimage to Chimayo.

Return to NM 76 and continue north up and down the hills. This is the most picturesque segment of the High Road to Taos. Each valley has a small village of farmers and woodcutters which dates back to Spanish colonial times. At the base of 13,102-foot Truchas Peak, Truchas (the name means "trout") was used in 1986 as the filming location for *The Milagro Beanfield War,* directed by Robert Redford from New Mexico author John Nichols' novel. Just off the highway at Las Trampas ("the traps") is an imposing mission church that dates back to 1751.

At Picurís (San Lorenzo) Pueblo, near the village of Peñasco, NM 76 ends in a T-intersection with NM 75. Secluded in its mountain valley, Picurís Pueblo has a restaurant, a fishing lake, and a small museum, where you can see examples of the unusual micaceous pottery that has been made here for 800 years. Mica in the local clay gives the pots an iridescent, almost bronzelike appearance. This pottery has recently become popular among Indian pottery collectors. While most residents of Picurís Pueblo live in government project housing, the ancient pueblo is being restored, and tours are available for a small fee.

From the highway intersection at Picurís, following the signs to Taos—turning right and then, 7 miles later, left on NM 518 through Carson National Forest—is the shorter (26 miles) but not much faster route. I suggest, instead, that you turn left (west) on NM 75, which will take you down a continuous 17-mile descent to the Rio Grande, passing through the artists-and-apple-orchards community of Dixon. When you return to NM 68, turn right (north) and go 10 miles to Pilar. Turn left, following the sign to Orillo Verde Recreation Area (formerly Rio Grande State Park). A $2 day-use fee is charged for picnicking in the park but not for driving through. The road follows the riverbank up the gorge, past several picnic areas. When the pavement ends, turn right (east). The road climbs out of the canyon, affording a good view of the Taos Valley with Wheeler Peak (at 13,161 feet, the highest mountain in New Mexico) in the background. Soon the pavement resumes and zips you back to the main highway just south of Ranchos de Taos. (Note: At press time, the unpaved portion of the Orillo Verde road was closed due to flood damage, and plans to reopen it were indefinite. The alternative is to stay on NM 68 all the way to Taos.)

A congested 3-mile commercial strip leads to the historic district. Turn left at the top of the block-long hill to reach the pretty, modernized town plaza.

Taos Sightseeing Highlights

Kit Carson Home and Museum—On Kit Carson Road (Highway 64) just across the main highway from the plaza area, this 12-room adobe was Kit Carson's home for 25 years from 1843 to 1868. It houses a museum of territorial period antiques and a small chapel. Open daily from 8:00 a.m. to 6:00 p.m. during the summer months, 9:00 a.m. to 5:00 p.m. the rest of the year; admission $5 for adults, $3 for senior citizen and for children under 12, maximum $10 per family. The same admission also includes the Blumenschein House and the Martinez Hacienda. Kit Carson's grave is two blocks to the north in the park named after him.

Blumenschein Home—On Ledoux Street one block south of the plaza, this 1797 adobe house was the home and studio of Ernest Blumenschein, a founder in 1915 of the Taos Society of Artists. Changing art exhibits, European antiques, and handmade Taos furniture are on display. Open daily from 9:00 a.m. to 5:00 p.m.; combined admission with the Kit Carson Home (see above) and the Martinez Hacienda.

Martinez Hacienda—This is the only remaining Spanish colonial hacienda in New Mexico open to the public on a regular basis. Built in 1804 as a fortresslike refuge from Comanche raids, it has thick adobe walls and no exterior windows. To find it, follow Ranchitos Road west from the plaza until you reach the Rio Grande. The 21-room hacienda is on the riverbank. Open daily from 9:00 a.m. to 5:00 p.m.; combined admission with the Kit Carson Home and the Blumenschein Home (above).

Taos Pueblo—The oldest and best-known of the Rio

Grande Indian pueblos, now a National Historic Landmark, this pueblo preserves the multistory architectural style that dates back to the 12th century. About 1,400 people live in the pueblo today. Ceremonies and dances held at the pueblo include the Fiesta of San Antonio on June 13, a corn dance in late June, a three-day powwow in early July, and the Fiesta of San Geronimo on the evening of September 29 and all day September 30. Call the pueblo at (505) 758-8626 for more information. To reach the pueblo, continue north from the plaza on NM 68 for about 2 miles and watch for the turnoff on your right. Open to the public daily from 8:00 a.m. to 6:00 p.m. during the summer months, 9:00 a.m. to 4:30 p.m. the rest of the year. A $5 parking fee is charged, and photography fees are $5 for still cameras and $10 for movie or video cameras; no cameras are allowed during ceremonies.

Millicent Rogers Museum—Founded in 1953 and relocated to its present building in 1968, this museum houses one of the most extensive private collections of Indian art in the Southwest. Featured are Navajo and Pueblo jewelry, Navajo textiles, Pueblo pottery and paintings, Hopi and Zuñi kachinas, and basketry from several Native American cultures as well as some Spanish colonial folk art items. To get there, go 4 miles north of Taos on the main highway, turn left just before the blinking light and follow the signs. Open daily from 9:00 a.m. to 5:00 p.m.; admission $6 for adults, $5 for students and senior citizens, $1 for children ages 6 to 16, maximum $12 per family.

D. H. Lawrence Ranch—The British novelist, whose books stirred controversy on both sides of the Atlantic, took refuge here during 1924-25 to escape public notoriety. His widow, Frieda, willed the ranch to the University of

New Mexico on condition that 10 acres of the property, including the ranch buildings and shrine, always remain open to the public. While Lawrence never wrote a major work with a New Mexico setting, writers and readers from all over the world visit to draw inspiration from the Lawrence Shrine. Lawrence's ashes may be blended into the concrete slab in the shrine. (Somebody's are, anyway. As the story goes, there was a mix-up of urns at U.S. Customs in New York when the ashes were being brought from France. An appropriate postscript to an enigmatic life.) To reach the ranch, take the marked turnoff on the left, about 7 miles north of Taos on NM 68. The shrine is 100 yards uphill from the visitor parking area.

Besides writing, Lawrence once tried his hand at the visual arts. Amateurish though his attempts may have been, his paintings scandalized London and resulted in an obscenity prosecution that drove him from England for the last time. You can view the naughty pictures and judge for yourself for $3 in a back room of La Fonda de Taos on the town plaza.

Rio Grande Gorge Bridge—The only bridge across the gorge, affording a spectacular view of this stretch of the Rio Grande protected under the federal Wild and Scenic Rivers Act, is on US 64 (the highway to Tres Piedras), about 10 miles west of the intersection with NM 68, which is 4 miles north of Taos.

Wild Rivers Recreation Area—This recreation area at the confluence of the Rio Grande and Red River 20 miles from Taos—turn left 3 miles north of Questa on NM 378 and follow the signs—has been the launching area for raft trips through the Taos Box on the Rio Grande for many years. It became so heavily used that in 1990, the federal government declared its new, official status and built a visitors center. Other amenities include hiking trails, hot springs by the river's edge, and campsites on the canyon rim. Camping costs $10; admission to the recreation area is free.

Lodging

One of the most interesting places to stay in Taos is the **Fechin Inn**, 227 Paseo de Pueblo Norte, (505) 751-1000. Located next to Kit Carson Park within easy walking distance of the plaza, this inn is decorated with many replicas of hand-carved wood detailing created by Russian-born Taos artist Nikolai Fechin. Rooms vary widely and range in price from $110 to $270 a night.

Another offbeat piece of Taos history is the **Laughing Horse Inn**, 729 Paseo del Pueblo Norte, (505) 758-8350. Once the home of author-publisher Spuds Johnson, who put out a literary magazine with a printing press in the back room, this bed and breakfast showcases many authentic details of old Taos adobe homes; some rooms even have traditional earthen floors that were drenched in ox blood and polished to a hard, durable shine. Here, too, rates vary widely, starting around $70.

Of the many Taos bed-and-breakfast inns, perhaps the most elegant is the **Mabel Dodge Luhan House**, 240 Morada Lane, (505) 751-9686. Luhan, a wealthy New York heiress, came to Taos in the 1920s with her third husband, whom she soon dumped in favor of Tony Luhan, an Indian from Taos Pueblo. She reigned as the patroness of the burgeoning Taos arts community through the 1940s and is primarily responsible for establishing the town's international status as an arts center.

The **Historic Taos Inn**, 125 Paseo del Pueblo Norte,

(505) 758-2233, dates back to the late 1800s and is a National Historic Landmark. Close to the plaza, this intimate inn has a tree-shaded interior courtyard and a greenhouse whirlpool spa surrounded by plants. Rooms vary widely, with rates from $60 to $270.

Budget lodging is hard to find in Taos, but if you're counting pennies you might want to drive several miles north of town on Taos Ski Valley Road to the **Abominable Snowmansion**, (505) 776-2422, a hostel where units with four or more bunk beds each can be rented on a dormitory basis or as private rooms. There are also several real teepees for rent and a ranch-style bunkhouse dorm.

Food

Taos boasts more than 50 restaurants—an astonishing number for a town of only 9,000 people. Good American, New Mexican, and Italian food can be found just off the plaza at the **Garden Restaurant**, North Plaza, (505) 758-9483, serving breakfast, lunch, and dinner every day. Also recommended is the **Apple Tree Restaurant**, 123 Bent Street, (505) 758-1900, with imaginative fare such as mango beef enchiladas.

Homey little local favorites include **Michael's Kitchen**, 304-C Paseo del Pueblo Norte, (505) 758-4178, serving up hamburgers and northern New Mexico specialties in rustic surroundings.

You'll also find traditional New Mexican cooking at **Roberto's**, 121½ Kit Carson Road, (505) 758-2434, across the street from the Kit Carson Home. Dinner only.

One of the long-standing favorite restaurants in town is **Doc Martin's** in the Historic Taos Inn, 125 Paseo del

Pueblo Norte, (505) 758-1977, with a changing menu of fine Southwest nouveau cuisine ranging from lamb to wild game and live, sometimes overwhelming, dinnertime jazz.

A former chef at Doc Martin's started his own restaurant more than a decade ago. **Lambert's of Taos**, 309 Paseo del Pueblo Sur, (505) 758-1009, is a strong contender for the title of finest dining establishment in town. Fresh seafood is a specialty. Unlike Doc Martin's, Lambert's is open for dinner only.

Camping

The prettiest places to camp in the vicinity of Taos include **Wild Rivers Recreation Area**, 20 miles north of town on a bluff overlooking the Rio Grande, and **Santa Barbara Campground** near Peñasco, about 20 miles south of Taos on the High Road, where you'll find crowds, creekside campsites, and a Pecos Wilderness trailhead.

Hiking, Biking, and Rafting

The most popular thrill sport in the Taos area (besides skiing at New Mexico's largest ski area) is whitewater rafting down the Taos Box—another name for the Rio Grande Gorge, the wild canyon you see from the Gorge Bridge. All-day raft trips put in at Wild Rivers Recreation Area north of Taos and pull out at Pilar, south of Taos. The many raft trip operators in town include **Far Flung Adventures**, El Prado, (505) 758-2628; **Los Rios River Runners**, Ski Valley Road, (505) 776-8854; and **Native Sons Adventures**, 715 Paseo del Pueblo Sur, (505) 758-9342.

One of the best hiking trails in the Taos area starts at

Santa Barbara Campground near Peñasco, on the High Road to Taos, and goes through the Pecos Wilderness for 12 miles to the summit of Truchas Peak.

Between Ranchos de Taos and Peñasco, several primitive roads that are ideal for mountain biking turn off the High Road to Taos and lead through Carson National Forest.

Bookstores

Taos has two long-established independent bookstores:

Fernandez de Taos Bookstore, 109 North Taos Plaza, (505) 758-4391.

Moby Dickens Bookshop, 124-A Bent Street, (505) 758-3050.

Great Sand Dunes National Park

A national monument since 1933, Great Sand Dunes was upgraded to national park status in 2000 by the same act of Congress that authorized federal acquisition of the Valles Caldera (see Day 9). While it's true that the dunes are one of the Southwest's most spectacular natural features, it is not the spectacular dune field that is the reason for the upgrade, but the adjacent ranchland with its varied ecosystem of marshes, meadowlands, and forest. Underneath this land are natural aquifers that contain large quantities of water. The purchase of this land protects the aquifers from being drained to supply the rapidly growing Boulder–Denver–Colorado Springs area to the northeast. National park status may also open the area adjoining the sand dunes to hotel development or other concessions.

Suggested Schedule

9:00 a.m.	Breakfast in Taos.
10:00 a.m.	Drive north, visiting San Luis and Fort Garland en route.
1:00 p.m.	Arrive at Great Sand Dunes in time to be

sure of getting a campsite. If you're not camping, check in to your Alamosa area lodging first and then drive out to the Sand Dunes when the temperature begins to cool down.

Travel Route: Taos to Great Sand Dunes National Park (130 miles)

From Taos, continue north on NM 522 (which becomes CO 159 as it crosses the state line) for 79 miles, following the Sangre de Cristo Mountains along the eastern side of the San Luis Valley through San Luis, Colorado's oldest town, founded in 1851. The small museum and cultural center in San Luis contains an excellent exhibit, funded by the National Endowment for the Humanities, explaining the history of the valley and its people. Also worth visiting is the ¾-mile trail that leads to a hilltop pilgrims' shrine, with almost life-size bronze sculptures depicting the stations of the cross along the way. CO 159 joins US 160 near Fort Garland, an 1850s U.S. Army outpost once commanded by Kit Carson and now a Colorado State Historic Site. This route is known as the Kit Carson Highway.

Though just up the river from Taos, the San Luis Valley wasn't explored by the Spanish for nearly two centuries. In 1779, the conquistador De Anza braved Comanche war parties to make it as far as Alamosa, where the Rio Grande veers west to its headwaters in the San Juan Mountains. The discovery astonished mapmakers of the time, who had always assumed that the river came from the North Pole. U.S. Army occupation in the mid-1800s made the valley safe for Hispanic settlers, whose descendants live there today.

From Fort Garland, turn left (west) on US 160 and go 10 miles to the turnoff on the right (north) to Great Sand Dunes National Park. From there, it's 16 miles to the park entrance gate.

Sightseeing Highlights

Great Sand Dunes National Park—Like a beach in reverse, a wide shallow ribbon of cold mountain stream water lies along the edge of a vast and awesome expanse of sand. Beyond the picnic area turnoff near the visitors center, a mostly local crowd basks on beach towels beside beer coolers while the kids construct sand castles along the creek. It could be time to break out the bathing suits, even though the water is only two inches deep.

The sand dunes, the largest in the United States, formed as millennia of sandstorms swept the San Luis Valley, as they still do, dropping their loads of sand in a pile where the wind funnels into the mountains. The dunes are 900 feet high and cover an area of 60 square miles. To get a sense of how big the dunes really are, take out your binoculars and watch tiny hikers struggle toward the summits. For an even better sense, climb one yourself (allow two hours up, half an hour back) and, when you finally reach the top, you'll be rewarded by a view of many more miles of sand. A less crowded dune area is reached by a trail that leads from the campground past where escape dunes have engulfed the ponderosa forest.

Often used as an "alien planet" location for science-fiction movies, the dunes also offer incomparable photographic opportunities. Particularly in early morning and late afternoon as shadows deepen, their weird abstractions challenge the eye. No two photographers' pictures of the sand dunes look alike. When hiking on the sand, wrap your camera in a plastic bag to protect the lens and mechanism from grit.

Entrance to the park is $5 unless you have a National Parks Pass. Open year-round.

San Luis Valley Alligator Farm—Alligators are about the last thing you'd expect to find in this desert valley where winter temperatures are among the coldest in Colorado, but here they are, west of Great Sand Dunes National Park on CO 17 between Mosca and Hooper. With its tropically warm pools fed by 87-degree geothermal springs, the farm began as a facility for raising tilapia, but as the fish were cleaned for commercial sale, the owners found that disposing of the guts after cleaning was a problem. They solved it by bringing in the alligators, which have become a tourist attraction. Open daily from 7:00 a.m. to 7:00 p.m. in summer, 10:00 a.m. to 3:00 p.m. the rest of the year. Admission is $5 for adults, $2.50 for children ages 6 to 12.

Lodging

Alamosa, 32 miles from Great Sand Dunes, is your best bet for motel accommodations. The **Best Western Alamosa Inn**, 1919 Main Street, (719) 589-2567, has an indoor pool; doubles start at $79 in summer, $69 off-season. The **Holiday Inn**, 333 Santa Fe Avenue, (719) 589-5833, also has an indoor pool as well as a sauna and whirlpool; rates start at $78. Lower-priced lodging can be found at the **Days Inn**, 2240 O'Keefe Parkway, (719) 589-9037; doubles start at $49 in season, $35 off-season. All three motels have cable color television.

The **Cottonwood Bed & Breakfast & Gallery**, 123 San Juan Avenue, (719) 589-3882, in Alamosa offers five guest rooms, each with private bath, in a beautifully restored turn-of-the-century home. Works by San Luis Valley artists grace the guest rooms and parlor; $65 to $90 including a lavish gourmet breakfast.

Food

I hope you brought some. Otherwise, a limited selection of groceries and microwave sandwiches is available at the **Great Sand Dunes Oasis** store. The nearest restaurant to Great Sand Dunes is the unpretentious little no-name road-side café at Fort Garland.

For fine dining with a view of the dunes, head for the **Great Sand Dunes Country Inn at Zapata Ranch**, 5303 Route 150, Mosca, (719) 378-2356, just west of the park. Zapata Ranch is one of the largest commercial buffalo ranches in the state, so naturally enough the restaurant specializes in bison steaks and roasts.

In Alamosa, budget-priced traditional dishes of the San Luis Valley (similar to northern New Mexico food except for a different style of green chile sauce) are served at **Mrs. Rivera's Kitchen**, 1019 West Sixth Street, (719) 589-0277.

Camping

The 88-site **Pinyon Flats Campground** at Great Sand Dunes National Park has tables, fire grills, convenient rest rooms, and nightly campfire talks. All campsites have fine views of the dunes. Deer are abundant and may bound right through your camp. The campground area also teems with chipmunks, ground squirrels, and cottontail rabbits.

Both the dunes trail and the Medano Pass Primitive Road that intersects it are ideal for sunset walking. No hookups.

Full hookups are available at the **Great Sand Dunes Oasis** outside the park. They also offer horseback riding and four-wheel-drive tours into the backcountry dunes.

Within the park, backcountry camping is allowed (free permit required, campfires prohibited) at Sand Pit and Castle Creek, 1½ and 2 miles up Medano Creek Primitive Road. Unless you have four-wheel drive, don't even think of driving on this road—the minimum tow charge for getting unstuck from the sand is upwards of $100. If you're fully equipped for backpacking, there is a hikers-only campground a quarter-mile from the road at mile 4.

Hiking and Biking

Climbing the nearest of the Great Sand Dunes is the best hiking challenge in the area. Some adventure-seekers have also discovered other ways to play in the sand, such as sliding down their slopes on saucer sleds or thick sheets of plastic (don't try this when the sand is hot). Some cross-country skiers have found that the dunes are also suitable for telemark skiing. Surprisingly, the sand causes minimal damage to skis.

Bookstores

You'll find regional books in Alamosa at:

Autumn Harvest Books, 620 Main Street, (719) 589-4987.

Narrow Gauge Newsstand, 602 Main Street, (719) 589-6712.

Durango

Since you left Albuquerque, you've followed the Rio Grande north for over 250 miles. Today you'll head west across the Great Divide to the Four Corners region, so called because the conjunction of Colorado, New Mexico, Arizona, and Utah—marked by a small monument (which isn't worth going out of your way for) beside US 160 an hour's drive southwest of Mesa Verde—is the only place in the United States where four states meet. Durango is the region's major town and tourism center. You'll spend most of today driving there.

Durango, a lively town of about 12,000 people, got its start in 1880 as a rail hub serving local ranches as well as gold and silver mines in the mountains to the north. Today, Durango thrives on tourism. The downtown historic district, centered around the Durango & Silverton Narrow Gauge (D&SNG) railroad station and the Strater Hotel, has been prettified far beyond its original Victorian splendor. Besides being close to Mesa Verde, Durango attracts year-round tourism with its famous narrow gauge railroad, Purgatory ski area (which has an alpine slide in the summertime), the annual Iron Horse Bicycle Race, rafting, fishing, cross-country skiing, and a host of other outdoor recreation possibilities.

In recent years, Durango has attracted an impressive number of fine artists and craftspeople, whose creations can be seen in at least 15 galleries and shops on and near Main Avenue between Fifth and Eleventh streets. The Durango Arts Center at 970 Main Avenue (970) 259-2606, exhibits works by local artists and serves as a ticket outlet for the performing arts in the area.

Suggested Schedule

8:00 a.m.	Hike the Great Sand Dunes in the cool of the morning.
10:00 a.m.	Drive to Antonito.
11:30 a.m.	Drive to Chama, stopping for a picnic on Cumbres Pass
3:00 p.m.	Drive to Durango. Check in to your lodging. Visit the railroad museum. Watch the train pull in.
4:30 p.m.	Leisurely stroll around town before dinner.

Travel Route: Sand Dunes to Durango—Direct (185 miles) or Scenic (217 miles)

Leaving Great Sand Dunes National Monument by the same 16-mile road you came in on, turn right (west) on US 160 and drive 16 more miles into Alamosa (pop. 7,000), the largest town in the San Luis Valley. There, at the junction of US 160 and US 285, you face a choice.

Durango lies on the other side of the Continental Divide, at the southwestern edge of the San Juan Mountains, the massive range you see to the west. The well-

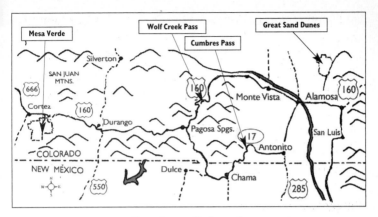

Southern Colorado

trodden tourist trail from Alamosa to Durango follows US 160 the whole way, about a 4-hour drive. The main scenic attraction on the route, and at the same time the major drawback, is 10,850-foot Wolf Creek Pass. Legendary among truck drivers, it's Colorado's highest and steepest mountain pass on a major highway. On the ascent, you may see (or join) numerous tourist vehicles overheated by the roadside. The long runaway-truck ramp on the descent is there for a reason: be very careful not to "ride" your car's brakes, which will overheat them and cause them to fail. This pass can pose a formidable obstacle to motor homes. Traffic may distract you from the scenery.

I suggest you try the much less traveled route over La Manga and Cumbres passes (10,230 feet and 10,022 feet). While these twin passes aren't much lower than Wolf Creek, the climb is more gradual. The relaxing drive through high mountain meadows is worth the extra 1½ hours of driving time. From Alamosa, turn left and follow US 285 straight south to Antonito (28 miles). Turn right (west) on State

Highway 17 toward Chama. The highway climbs up from the San Luis Valley into San Juan National Forest, first following the Conejos River past a series of campgrounds and fishing spots, then ascending into the alpine meadows. At the top you'll see the tracks of the Cumbres & Toltec Scenic Railroad, which runs between Antonito and Chama by a different route. At the far end of the grassy slopes, just before you begin your descent, stand the train station, snowshed, and other abandoned buildings of Cumbres, a railroad ghost town from the 1880s. Descend into New Mexico. The road distance from Antonito to Chama is 48 miles.

At the junction about a mile south of Chama, just a few miles over the state line, turn right on US 84, which climbs back up into the national forest to Pagosa Springs, Colorado, 49 miles away. There, rejoin US 160 westbound to Durango (60 miles). Mesa Verde National Park is 36 miles past Durango on US 160.

Sightseeing Highlights

The scenic drive described above is today's top sight. If you have an extra day to explore southern Colorado, take one of the two old-fashoined narrow-gauge steam train trips that carry visitors over the mountains and into the past:

Cumbres & Toltec Scenic Railroad—This train runs from Antonito to the 19th-century ghost town of Osier on the Colorado-New Mexico state line, where it meets a different steam train that goes between the state line and Chama, New Mexico. Especially popular during fall colors season, it's an all-day round-trip with spectacular views of the Sangre de Cristo Mountains to the east and the San Juan Mountains to the west. For the trip from Antonito to Osier and back, the cost is $38 per adult, $35 for seniors and $19 for children under 12. (The same prices apply for round-trips between Chama and Osier.) Or you can ride all the way from Antonito to Chama, switching trains at Osier, with a return shuttle, for $58 per adult, $47 for seniors and $29 for children. Reservations are highly recommended. Call (719) 376-5483 in Antonito or (505) 756-2151 in Chama.

Durango & Silverton Narrow Gauge Railroad—The most famous old-time steam train in the Rockies runs between Durango and the old mining/lumbering town of Silverton high in the San Juan Mountains, round-trip only. Along the way, it follows the Animas River Canyon, sometimes inching its way across the face of nearly sheer cliffs, as a guide tells tales of former mining days in the San Juans. The D&SNG is one of Colorado's most popular tourist attractions, and reservations should be made months in advance if possible by calling (970) 247-2733 or (888) 872-4607. Up to four trains run daily, 45 minutes apart, during the summer, two a day during fall colors season, and a daily train goes as far as Cascade Canyon during the winter. The round-trip to Silverton takes about nine hours; trains start arriving back in Durango a little before 5:00 p.m. Fares are $53 for adults, $27 for children ages 5 to 11. There's also a luxury parlor car, costing $88 per person.

The Durango & Silverton Railroad Museum, located in the old roundhouse beside the Durango depot, 479 Main Avenue, has steam engines, passenger coaches, and photographs telling the story of the railroad from 1882 to the present day. Admission is $5 for adults, $2.50 for children.

Lodging

Durango has an abundance of hotels and motels in all price ranges. The finest is the **Strater Hotel,** the four-story brick centerpiece of downtown Durango's historic restoration district, at 699 Main Avenue, (970) 247-4431. Dating back to 1887, the Strater has been undergoing room-by-room restoration for over 20 years. Guest rooms feature antique walnut furnishings, and public areas include a playhouse where melodramas are performed from June through September and an elegant Old West saloon; doubles start at $130 in season, $70 off-season.

While the Strater has a more authentic patina of age, many Durango visitors prefer the **General Palmer Hotel,** a block down the street at 567 Main Avenue, (970) 247-4747. With shiny brass fittings, period reproduction furniture, and a front parlor full of teddy bears, this Victorian-era historic hotel seems both old and, at the same time, new; rates start at $100 in season, $75 off-season.

A smaller historic hostelry away from the busy main street is the **Rochester Hotel,** 726 East Second Avenue, (970) 385-1920. Originally a 30-room boarding house, the walls between some units have been removed to make just 15 spacious luxury guest rooms. The decor features movie posters and memorabilia recalling Hollywood westerns that have been filmed in the Durango area; rooms start at $140 a night in season.

Moderately priced motels are concentrated along North Main Avenue (US 550 northbound). Good bets are the **Caboose Motel,** 3363 N. Main Avenue, (970) 247-1191, with $50 to $70 doubles; the **Siesta Motel,** 3475 N. Main Avenue, (970) 247-0741, with doubles starting at $55 in summer and as low as $30 the rest of the year; and the **Alpine Motel**, 3515 N. Main Avenue, (970) 247-4042, where rooms start at $60 in season, as low as $38 off-season.

Food

It costs less than you might expect to dine in a Victorian atmosphere at **Henry's Chophouse & Italian Bistro**, the Strater Hotel's restaurant, 699 Main Avenue, (970) 247-4431. Steak or seafood dinners range between $10 and $20. Following this 22-day itinerary, you won't find another restaurant in the Southwest as splurge-worthy as this one until you arrive back in Las Vegas.

The **Palace Grill**, located next to the narrow-gauge train station at 505 Main Avenue, (970) 247-2018, offers dishes such as honey duck and brandy pepper steak in a Victorian-style setting. They serve lunch and dinner Monday through Friday; Saturday dinner only; Sunday lunch only.

Francisco's Restaurante y Cantina, 619 Main Avenue, (970) 247-4098, has been operated for more than 30 years by a family from northern New Mexico. It's one of Durango's largest and most popular restaurants, serving lunch and dinner daily.

In small-town Colorado, "seafood" is generally synonymous with trout. A notable exception is **Red Snapper**, 144 East Ninth Street, (970) 259-3417, where you'll find a full range of seafood including Australian lobster tails, New Orleans-style shrimp, scallops Dijonaise, and an oyster bar.

For healthy breakfast specials, try the **Carver Bakery, Café and Brewpub**, 1022 Main Avenue, (970) 259-2545. They also serve lunch, dinner, freshly ground gourmet coffee, and homemade beer.

Harley Davidson memorabilia set the stage for giant hamburgers at the **Scootin' Blues Café and Lounge,** 900 Main Avenue, (970) 259-1400, which also features live blues bands five nights a week.

Camping

The closest public campgrounds to Durango are nine national forest campgrounds on the shores of Vallecito Reservoir, about 25 miles northeast of town (take slow, two-lane blacktop CO 3 from Durango or drive east on US 160 to Bayfield and turn north). They range in size from **Miller Campground** (11 sites) to **Vallecito Campground** (80 sites), and there are no hookups at any of them. Vallecito Campground has a trailhead into the Weminuche Wilderness as well as shorter nature trails.

For pleasant lakefront campsites with a panoramic mountain view, head for **Lake Mancos State Recreation Area,** located near the town of Mancos and the turnoff for Mesa Verde National Park. No hookups.

There are also several high-altitude, short-season (mid-June through August) national forest campgrounds, which fill up fast, along the San Juan Skyway between Durango and Silverton.

Hiking and Biking

The San Juan Mountains north of Durango, the most majestic in the Colorado Rockies, are often likened to the Swiss Alps. Most of these mountains lie within federally designated wilderness areas accessible only on foot, horseback, or in winter, cross-country skis.

An extensive network of trails through the wilderness is accessible from trailheads along US 550 between Durango and Ouray. Try the **Cascade Creek Trail,** which runs 4 miles (one-way) down from the highway to join the **Animas River Trail,** a major wilderness artery. Many hikers say the best trek in the San Juans is the **Needle Creek Trail,** a 14-mile (one-way) hike through the Chicago Basin leading to a cluster of three 14,000-foot mountain peaks in the heart of the San Juan Wilderness; the trail can be reached easily only from a whistlestop trailhead along the Durango & Silverton Narrow Gauge train route. Another train will stop to pick you up on the return trip.

Mountain bikes are not permitted in the designated wilderness areas of the San Juans, but there are plenty of old mining roads in the mountains north of Durango that make for fantastic biking. The chair lift at Purgatory Ski Area (US 550, 970-247-9000) north of Durango operates in the summer to carry riders and their bikes to the summit, where they can ride the 4-mile **Parris Park Loop** across the alpine Hermosa Creek Valley on the back side of the mountain. A longer and more challenging ride, the **Hermosa Creek Trail** (23 miles) takes cyclists through high meadows and along the rim of the Hermosa Cliffs.

Bookstores

Look for books of local and regional interest in both Pagosa Springs and Durango at:

Wolftracks Bookstore & Coffee Co., 135-A Country Center Drive, Pagosa Springs, (970) 731-6020.

The Bookcase, 601 East Second Avenue, Durango, (970) 247-3776.

Maria's Bookshop, 960 Main Avenue, Durango, (970) 247-1438.

Mesa Verde National Park

Today you'll begin exploring the ruins left behind by the remote ancestors of the ancient and modern Pueblo Indians you saw in the Santa Fe–Los Alamos–Taos area. The Anasazi people thrived in the Four Corners area for seven centuries until, 800 years ago, they suddenly vanished from the region. Today, their monumental cliff dwellings at Mesa Verde are a popular, often crowded national park.

"Anasazi" is a Navajo word meaning "ancestors of our enemies" (the National Park Service translates it more politely as "ancient ones"). It is the name given to the ancestors of the Pueblo Indians who lived in the Four Corners area until the 12th century. Of several distinct Anasazi groups, the three largest were the Mesa Verde and Chaco cultures, whose cities you'll see today and tomorrow, and the Kayenta people who built the cliff dwellings at Navajo National Monument (Day 16).

The Anasazi lived at the northernmost reach of trade routes established by the Toltecs and other great civilizations of Mexico, so they learned agricultural, architectural, and other technologies much earlier than did tribes in other parts of northern America. Their religion, too, evolved from Mexican origins. From about the year 1000 on, the Anasazi had the largest cities north of the tropics on the American continent.

In the 12th century, within one or two generations, the Anasazi abandoned their pueblos one after another until the Four Corners area was virtually unpopulated. Nobody knows why. War? Disease? Drought? Wanderlust? Anthropologists argue endlessly. The current theory is that overpopulation brought soil depletion, erosion, and environmental disaster. The mysterious fall of the Anasazi empire is worthy of meditation among the ruins.

Suggested Schedule

8:30 a.m. Drive from Durango to Mesa Verde National Monument

10:00 a.m. Visit the museum and learn about the people who lived in these amazing cliff dwellings.

11:00 a.m. Walk the trail behind the museum into Spruce Tree Canyon.

1:00 p.m. Did you bring picnic supplies? If not, grab a quick bite at the snack bar near the museum or drive back to Far View Visitor Center, where there is a cafeteria.

Afternoon Rent a bicycle at the museum for a leisurely tour of the cliff dwellings on Chapin Mesa, then finish your day with a hike from the museum out to Petroglyph Point. Or, the less athletic may wish to tour Chapin Mesa by car and then return

to Far View Visitor Center for a trip out to
Wetherill Mesa.

Evening   Spend the night in the park or return to
Durango.

Sightseeing Highlights

Mesa Verde National Park—In 1906, when Mesa Verde
was made a national park to protect the largest and most
extensive cliff dwellings in North America, the rare horseback visitor must have found the experience of a lifetime.
Today its immense popularity, necessitating crowd control
to protect archaeological sites, channels many tourists into
a few public areas, making Mesa Verde a congested place.
Yet the magic of this piñon-covered island 2,000 feet in the
sky, with its ancient, castlelike "lost cities," makes itself
felt even in a crowd.

Start touring Mesa Verde early in the morning to beat
the charter buses. Admission to the park is $10 per vehicle.
A long, steep climb takes you to the mesa top. (Travel trail-
ers must be left below at the entrance station parking area
or at the campground.) Pause at Park Point, with its superb
view of the Mancos and Montezuma valleys and the San
Juan Mountains. Midway along the park road you'll come
to Far View Visitor Center, where you can find the current
schedule for ranger-guided walks. One of these walks,
offered free by the National Park Service, can enhance your
Mesa Verde experience with insights about the people who
once lived here and the plants and animals that still do.

Mesa Verde Museum—This old stone museum at park
headquarters on Chapin Mesa, 20 miles from the park
entrance, contains dioramas that show how civilization

evolved on Mesa Verde during the same time period as Europe's Dark Ages. Take time to admire the museum's collection of ancient pottery, with its fine craftsmanship and elaborate geometric designs, and appreciate the thousand-year artistic heritage behind the Pueblo pottery you saw (and may have bought) in Albuquerque, Santa Fe, and Taos. The museum is open daily from 8:00 a.m. to 5:00 p.m., free.

Chapin Mesa Ruins—Two separate loop roads begin at the museum on Chapin Mesa. Each road is about 3 miles round-trip and worth taking your time. Rent a bicycle at the museum, and the tour will seem even more spectacular. The major cliff dwellings are on the west loop, a left turn not far past the museum parking area. Of the many sites, Cliff Palace is the largest. It is accessible on a half-mile trail with a 500-foot climb; allow an hour. The walk to Balcony House, on the same road as it loops around to the other side of the mesa, means climbing a 32-foot ladder, ducking through a 12-foot tunnel, and ascending 100 feet up the cliff face. During crowded times, you can only see these two ruins on ranger-guided tours, which run frequently. The tour is well worth the wait.

Wetherill Mesa—A 20-mile drive from the Far View Visitor Center leads to recently excavated mesa-top pueblo ruins. The area could only be reached by shuttle bus until recently but is now open to automobiles, a move the park service hopes will alleviate traffic congestion in the main ruins area on Chapin Mesa. Keep your eyes peeled for wild horses along the way.

Food and Lodging

Far View Lodge in Mesa Verde is midway along the park road near Far View Visitor Center. Rates are about $100 in season, $90 off-season, the views are magnificent, and there is a good restaurant at the lodge as well as a cafeteria at the visitors center. For current prices and reservations, contact ARAMARK Mesa Verde Company, (800) 449-2288 or www.visitmesaverde.com.

Camping

Morefield Campground in Mesa Verde National Park is located 5 miles up the steep road from the park entrance. It's a huge campground—177 tent sites, 300 trailer/RV sites. Besides all the usual campground amenities, there are pay showers nearby at the grocery store. Campfire programs are presented nightly. The Knife Edge Trail, which starts at the edge of the campground, takes you out to a cliff view point ideal for sunset watching. Returning in the dusk, you're likely to see dozens of deer grazing in the meadow.

If the campground at Mesa Verde is full or you'd prefer to sleep alongside fewer campers, at **Lowry Ruins Historic Site** you may find yourself all alone. Operated by the Bureau of Land Management, the site is not marked on most road maps and is known to only the most dedicated Indian ruins buffs. There is no admission or camping fee, no ranger on duty, and no water, so be sure you have plenty aboard. To get to Lowry Ruins, continue on US 160 10 miles beyond the Mesa Verde turnoff to the town of Cortez, and from there go north 19 miles on US 666 to Pleasant View, where a small road goes west (left) 9 miles to the ruins.

Hiking and Biking

If you want to escape the crowds at Mesa Verde, walk. Two trails begin at the museum, where you must obtain a free hiking permit. The permit system and many visitors' aversion to physical exercise keep the trails uncrowded—only one out of a thousand visitors hikes either trail. **Spruce Canyon Trail** is 2.1 miles long with a 700-foot climb down and back. **Petroglyph Point Trail** is 2.3 miles long with no steep climbing. Either takes about two hours round-trip.

Off-road biking is not permitted in the national park. The loop road around Chapin Mesa can be surprisingly tranquil, though, especially in early morning or late afternoon when there is less traffic. Bicycles are available for rent at the museum on Chapin Mesa.

Aztec and Chaco Canyon

Today's journey takes you to Anasazi ruins larger, more remote, and even more mysterious than those at Mesa Verde. If you are equipped to camp and have at least a day's worth of food aboard, you can take time to explore Chaco Canyon, the Southwest's largest and strangest Indian ruin, and let your imagination run free. (Otherwise, you'll have to speed up today's sightseeing in order to reach Interstate 40, where the nearest motels are, by nightfall.)

Suggested Schedule

9:30 a.m.	Drive south from Durango to Aztec. (Start an hour earlier if you spent last night at Mesa Verde National Park.)
10:00 a.m.	See Aztec Ruins National Monument.
11:30 a.m.	Drive to Chaco Canyon.
2:00 p.m.	Arrive at Chaco Canyon. Stake out a campsite.
2:30 p.m.	Explore Chaco Canyon.
Evening	Camp at Chaco Canyon.

Travel Route: Mesa Verde to Chaco Canyon (132 miles)

From Mesa Verde National Park, return to Durango on US 160. Five miles east of Durango, where the highway forks, take US 550 south to Aztec. The total driving time from Mesa Verde to Aztec is 1½ hours.

The town of Aztec, population 6,000, won the National Municipal League's "All-American City" title in 1963 for building a 14-mile road to Navajo Lake—without help from any level of government. All funds, labor, and machinery were donated by local citizens. Aztec still takes the title to heart. A walk along the main street, with its small turn-of-the-century historic district and quaint local museum, can make you feel as if you'd slipped through time into Middle America, circa 1963.

Aztec Ruins National Monument is near the river, just over the bridge from downtown Aztec on the road to Farmington, plainly marked with signs.

Fill up with gas and check your food supply before leaving Aztec; you won't see another town until tomorrow. Drive south on NM 44 through the neighboring community of Bloomfield and out into the empty San Juan Basin.

Eighteen miles south of Aztec (13 miles past Bloomfield) on the left (east), an unpaved road turns off to Angel Peak Recreation Area. Fifteen miles past the Angel Peak turnoff on NM 44 is Blanco Trading Post, where a clearly marked road turns off to the right (southwest) toward Chaco Culture National Historic Park. The road, unpaved and 30 miles long, will take an hour to drive under good road conditions. "Don't pave the road to Chaco Canyon" was an environmentalist rallying cry in the mid-1970s. The issue of paving the road has come

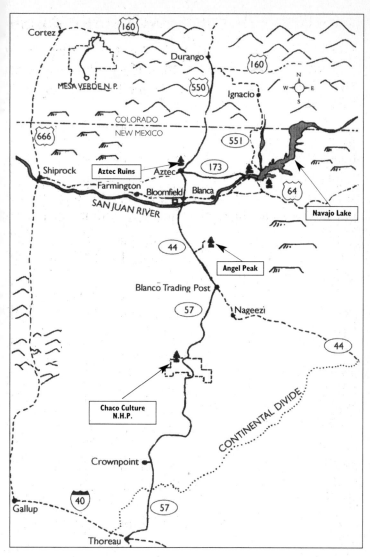

San Juan Basin

around again as Chaco Canyon has become better known and more visited. Still, while hordes of tourists overrun Mesa Verde, Chaco's park rangers can usually relax with a few dozen adventuresome visitors. The road is normally an easy drive, thrilling for a minute as it plunges headlong into the canyon to let you know you're almost there. If there have been recent thunderstorms in the area, call Chaco headquarters, (505) 786-5384, for a road condition report before proceeding. When wet, parts of the clay road can be as slick as a skating pond.

The surrounding land is sparsely inhabited by Navajo people. While not officially part of the reservation, most ranches in the area have been purchased by the tribe and are regarded as part of the Navajo Nation. There is no gasoline, food, lodging, or repair service at Chaco, and the nearest town is the one you just came from, 60 miles away.

Sightseeing Highlights

Aztec Ruins National Monument—Aztec Ruins, on the bank of the Animas River, was a large 12th-century pueblo. Its name derives from early settlers' mistaken belief that this and other southwestern ruins were colonies from a higher civilization in Mexico. While the Anasazi traded with Mexican Toltecs and perhaps Aztecs for parrots and other items, and some construction techniques apparently originated in Mexico, Aztec was actually built by colonists from Chaco, 60 miles to the south. Abandoned during the decline of the Chaco culture, the pueblo was later reoccupied by people from Mesa Verde. Artifacts and architectural features from both Anasazi cultures invite side-by-side comparison. The showpiece of this national monument is the fully reconstructed great kiva, which will help you appreciate other kiva ruins, such as Chaco's Casa Rinconada, as prehistoric cathedrals, not just big holes in the ground. The short (400-yard) path through the ruins is open from 8:00 a.m. to 5:00 p.m. daily all year and to 6:30 p.m. June through August. Admission is $4 per adult, free for those under 17.

If these ruins fascinate you, consider a one-hour side trip to **Salmon Ruins,** another colony of the Chacoan culture dating from the 11th century, 12 miles from Aztec on the road between Farmington and Bloomfield. Open 9:00 a.m. to 5:00 p.m. daily all year.

Navajo Lake—If you have extra time and a yearning for water, head for Navajo Lake, New Mexico's largest lake, near Aztec. Pine River Marina, 23 miles east of Aztec on NM 511 not far above the dam, has the nearest campground and boat rental. More remote facilities are at Sims Mesa across the lake; turn left at the first fork in the road after you cross the dam. Empty except on weekends, when the lake has been known to attract as many as 7,500 visitors at a time! Navajo Lake is a good place to rent a motorboat for a day or overnight back-canyon boat-camping trip.

Angel Peak Recreation Area—Here's a little-known, starkly beautiful spot with a free picnic and camping area. Angel Peak itself is easy to spot. It's the butte several miles to the east, crowned by a rock formation that, with imagination, resembles an angel with outspread wings. The sign marking the road that takes you there is less obvious. Drive in just half a mile to the first overlook and you'll be rewarded with a totally unexpected view of Kutz Canyon, a bright bit of red-and-white painted desert. There is a canyon rim picnic area 2½ miles farther down the road.

Chaco Culture National Historic Park—Until 1983, this site was called Chaco Canyon National Monument. Its official tongue twister name notwithstanding, most folks still just call it Chaco Canyon.

At Mesa Verde and Aztec, we can wonder why the Anasazi suddenly abandoned such beautiful spots. Chaco presents different archaeological mysteries. With so much wide open space around, why did the Chacoans cluster together into a mega-pueblo, the largest city the Anasazi ever saw, the Los Angeles of the prehistoric Southwest? And why, of all places, here?

Even with its sophisticated irrigation system, Chacoans could not grow enough food to support the population of 5,000 but had to import it from outlier colonies. For vigas, or roof and floor supports in the pueblos, the people had to carry countless thousands of ponderosa logs from the mountains 50 miles away, a formidable task considering that they had no horses, nor had they knowledge of the wheel. Chacoans' abundant turquoise supply came from even farther away, in the Cerrillos hills near Santa Fe. While they made elaborate and distinctive black-on-white decorative pottery, most everyday cooking pots were imported. What did they give in exchange for all the imports needed to keep this city alive?

Archaeologists don't know. A clue may lie in the extraordinary number of kivas at Chaco, which suggest that it was a religious center. Natural beauty, the spirit of place, was probably important in the religion of the Anasazi, as it is to their Pueblo descendants today. Especially at twilight, one can readily imagine Chaco Canyon as sacred land.

The largest pueblo, Pueblo Bonito, rose four stories and contained 800 rooms; it was the largest residential structure ever built before the 20th century. Besides all the excavated pueblos you see here, there are a number of others in the area that are crumbled and buried, recognizable only by differing vegetation. The Chaco people also established about 60 satellite pueblos called "outliers" throughout the San Juan Basin, from Aztec in the north to the Grants area in the south. The major outliers were connected by an 800-mile network of improved roads 30 feet wide, with Chaco at the hub.

Adding to the enigma of Chaco Canyon is the fact that, despite a large population apparently living here for several centuries, no human burials have ever been found here. Some experts hypothesize that the Chacoans actually made their homes in the outlying pueblos and traveled to Chaco for religious ceremonies or trade fairs. According to this theory, the large pueblos of Chaco might have been more analogous to today's big resort hotels than to apartment complexes.

Late afternoon or early morning is the best time to tour and photograph the ruins. For solitude and a different perspective on Chaco Canyon, hike the trail up to Tsin Kletsin ruins (4-mile, 2½-hour round-trip) on the canyon rim. The trail starts at Casa Rinconada, Chaco's largest great kiva.

Chaco Canyon is open year-round (road conditions permitting). Admission is $4 per vehicle.

Lodging and Food

The rustic three-room **Chaco Inn at the Post** is located at Nageezi Trading Post, about 3 miles north of the turnoff to Chaco; rates are in the $70 range. Otherwise, the closest motels to Chaco Canyon are in the Farmington-Bloomfield-

Aztec area and the Grants-Gallup area, each two hours away. The only campground is the one in the park. Bring your own food and firewood.

Camping

Chaco's **Gallo Campground** has only 47 established sites. A sign on the road into the park warns that the campground may fill up by 3:00 p.m. In fact, the park has become so popular in the last few years that the campground overflows almost every night, even off-season. Campers who arrive too late to obtain a site are permitted to park along a nearby gravel road—fine if you're in a self-contained RV, but a little rugged if you're pitching a tent. The campground has tables, fireplaces, and rest rooms. The only water supply is at the visitors center, about half a mile away. Rangers present campfire programs nightly during the summer season.

Angel Peak Recreation Area, south of Aztec (see above) has 16 beautifully situated, rarely used campsites with restrooms, picnic tables, and grills but no water.

Hiking and Biking

There are several backcountry hiking trails at Chaco. A free permit, obtained at the visitors center, is required. For solitude and a different perspective on Chaco Canyon, hike the trail up to **Tsin Kletsin** ruins on the canyon rim, a 4-mile, 2½-hour round-trip. The trail starts at Casa Rinconada, Chaco's largest great kiva.

There's good biking on both the level, paved park road and the long, flat unpaved roads outside the park boundary that lead to outliers such as Kin Ya'ah.

The Navajo Nation

The Navajo Nation encompasses nearly 16 million acres, an area larger than Connecticut, Massachusetts, and New Hampshire combined. The eastern part of the reservation is mountainous evergreen forest with several recreation lakes, the center is arid desert and piñon-covered red rock canyon country, and the western part is painted desert. All land on the reservation is inhabited—in fact, overpopulated, forcing the tribe to keep buying up private ranchland along its boundaries. This problem is not obvious because the Navajo traditionally locate each house out of sight of any other house.

Begin your tour of the largest Indian reservation in the United States with a visit to the tribal zoo and historic Hubbell Trading Post. You'll end the day at Canyon de Chelly, the heart of the land of the Navajo.

Suggested Schedule

9:00 a.m.   Leave Chaco Canyon.
11:00 a.m. Take a break in Gallup. Fill the gas tank, stock up on food, and continue to Window Rock.

Noon	Picnic at Window Rock Tribal Park.
1:00 p.m.	Visit the Navajo Tribal Zoo and the Navajo Nation Museum.
2:00 p.m.	Drive to Ganado.
2:30 p.m.	See Hubbell Trading Post.
3:15 p.m.	Drive to Canyon de Chelly National Monument.
4:00 p.m.	Arrive at Canyon de Chelly, find a camp site or check into the lodge, and visit the visitors center.
5:00 p.m.	Take a late afternoon drive along the north rim of Canyon del Muerto.

Travel Route: Chaco Canyon to Canyon de Chelly (156 miles)

The road south out of Chaco Canyon doesn't take as long to reach the pavement—just 10 dusty miles. Continue south and west on NM 57 as it joins the Vietnam Veterans Memorial Highway (NM 371) near Crownpoint and, 32 miles later, reaches I 40 at the tiny town of Thoreau, midway between Grants and Gallup.

Take the interstate west for 33 miles to Gallup, the "border town" of the Navajo Nation and the largest community in western New Mexico. Existing primarily as a truck stop and railroad way station, Gallup has an old downtown area on the south side of the interstate and train tracks and a strip of shopping malls, supermarkets, and fast-food places, as well as a city park full of big, colorful abstract sculptures, on the north side. On the old side, pawn shops, curio shops, and trading companies sell Navajo and Zuñi arts and crafts at prices far lower than

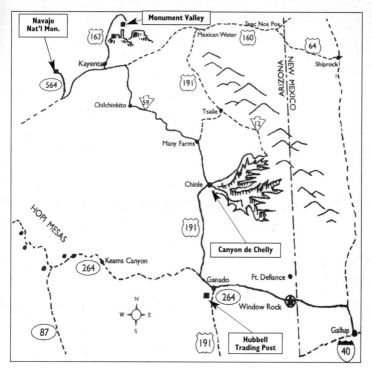

Navajoland

those in Albuquerque or Santa Fe. Some of the turn-of-the-century storefronts along Main Street have had recent face lifts to become galleries, but Gallup is a long way from becoming a touristy historic district. Restaurants and motels are, on the whole, budget-basic. Public intoxication is a common sight at any time of day or night because Gallup is the only place in the region where people can get a drink if they crave one. Alcoholic beverages are illegal on the Navajo Reservation and hard to get beyond the reservation's northern boundary, in Utah, where anything

187

stronger than beer is sold only in state liquor stores whose locations often seem like closely guarded secrets. This regrettable fact also makes the highway between Gallup and Window Rock one of the most dangerous roads in the Southwest after dark.

Take four-lane US 666 north from Gallup for 7 miles and turn west on Highway 264 to Window Rock, the Navajo Nation's capital (pop. 2,200). You will cross the Arizona state line shortly before entering town. Although the rest of Arizona stays on Mountain Standard Time while New Mexico, Colorado, and Utah observe Daylight Savings Time, the entire Navajo Nation also goes on Daylight Savings Time, so there is no need to reset your watch on this leg of the trip. (In fact, for the next few days there will be very little reason to consult your watch at all.)

From Window Rock, continue on Highway 264 for 34 more miles to reach Hubbell Trading Post, a mile past Ganado near the intersection with US 191. After visiting the trading post, turn north on US 191 and drive 31 miles to the turnoff for Chinle and Canyon de Chelly National Monument.

The Navajo Nation

Athabascan Indians gradually migrated from northwestern Canada to New Mexico and Arizona between the time when Mesa Verde and Chaco Canyon were abandoned and the time, five centuries later, when the Spanish came. Those who adopted new ways from the Pueblo people and Spanish settlers, such as sheepherding, weaving, and growing corn, came to be called Navajo (from a Pueblo word meaning "green planted fields"). The other Athabascans, who held to their older nomadic traditions, were called Apache.

In 1864, soon after the Navajo lands became U.S. territory (most reservation Navajo, young and old alike, talk as though it happened yesterday), Kit Carson's army burned the Navajo cornfields to starve the people out of hiding. Carson then marched the Navajo people, who then numbered about 8,000, along with 2,000 horses and 10,000 sheep and goats, for 300 miles to a camp at Fort Sumner in eastern New Mexico. Without supplies, many Navajo died along the trail. Famine plagued the Fort Sumner camps; meanwhile, American surveyors could find nothing desirable about the former Navajo lands. Four years later, the army marched the remaining Navajo and their flocks back home. The degrading experience fostered tribal unity, increased distrust of the Anglo, heightened belief in the special quality of their homeland, and galvanized the "Navajo Nation."

In a few scattered towns, 20th-century conveniences such as pickup trucks, video rental stores, and government housing projects adorned by satellite TV antennas—new additions to the tribe's unique way of life—have all been borrowed from the American mainstream. Horses, sheep, corn, jewelry making, and weaving were all similarly borrowed to create the traditional Navajo lifestyle, and the process continues.

The more you travel in Navajoland, the more it may seem like a Third World country (though one with exceptional respect for the natural environment). Most Navajo people speak their native language at home and usually speak English as a second language. Most Navajo people live away from towns and highways and have no electricity or running water. The tribe faces problems of poverty and overpopulation. The Navajo Nation, the largest tribe in the United States, now numbers about 200,000. Only 20 percent can live off the land, and of the rest, 85 percent are unemployed. Coal mines and natural gas wells provide tribal income and a few jobs, but scar the land. Experimental reservation industries range from a pilot microchip plant (now closed) to cultivation of rare oriental mushrooms.

You'll see signs on the reservation for three kinds of places that are central to Navajo society—trading posts, chapterhouses, and missions.

Trading posts are general stores operated by traders under federal license. They sell a selection of food somewhat more limited than 7-Eleven stores, as well as dry goods, gasoline, and sometimes hay or feed for livestock. Traditionally, traders also served as pawnbrokers, exchanging their wares for rugs and jewelry that they sold to collectors, and some trading posts continue the practice. If you stop at enough trading posts, you'll find a fair selection of Navajo handicrafts. For many Navajo it's a long trip to the trading post, and once there, they like to stay around for a good part of the day, talking with whoever else stops by.

Chapterhouses are the basic unit of Navajo tribal government. They serve the purpose of town meeting halls, even though many are far from any town. Chapters elect 88 councilmen to represent them in the tribal council. The Council Chambers, near Window Rock Tribal Park, are open from 8:00 a.m. to 5:00 p.m. on many weekdays. Visitors fortunate enough to find the council in session will hear tribal issues debated in both English and Navajo.

Missions have been established throughout the reservation by a number of Christian denominations. The first, at

Ganado, was built by the Presbyterians under a decree from President Grant which arbitrarily assigned Indian reservations to various missionary groups. Since the beginning of the 20th century, other missionaries have included the Franciscan Order and the Methodist and Christian Reformed churches. Visitors are welcome at all of them. Christian fundamentalist tent revivals, too, are held frequently around the reservation. Some feature Navajo preachers. If you come across one (audible for miles, they're hard to miss), by all means join the flock. Old-time evangelism among the Indians makes for a unique and thought-provoking cultural experience regardless of your personal faith. Despite more than a century of missionary efforts, however, few Navajo people are exclusively Christian. Traditional Navajo religious beliefs survive, and "sings"—healing ceremonies that involve chanting and sand painting—still take place, though non-Navajo visitors are rarely included.

Sightseeing Highlights

Window Rock Tribal Park—The rock formation for which the Navajo capital was named is a half-mile east (right) off Tribal Route 12 and a half-mile north of Arizona 264, at the end of the road that leads past the tribal administration buildings. Water from the springs in the park are considered sacred and have been used by Navajo shamanic healers for centuries. There are picnic tables, rest rooms, water, and a walking trail.

Navajo Tribal Zoological Park—This low-budget zoo looks like a combination barnyard and humane society shelter, but don't let first impressions put you off. Here you'll feel the Navajo people's unique attitude toward animals. Sheep and other domestic animals roam throughout the grounds, while wild animals (most were found injured and brought here from other parts of the reservation) are kept in wire pens to protect them from tourists. Signs name each animal in both English and Navajo, and a display in the visitors center tells a little bit about the animals' mythological roles as spiritual forefathers of the various Navajo clans. Among the zoo's residents are a black bear, a mountain lion, a wolf, birds of prey, and sometimes bison. Located off Arizona 264, a half-mile east of Window Rock Shopping Center, the zoo is open daily from 8:00 a.m. to 5:00 p.m.; 50 cents per person donation requested.

Navajo Nation Museum—Changing exhibits depict Navajo history and ways of life. There are also Anasazi artifacts and a large arts and crafts shop. On AZ 264 between the shopping center and Window Rock Motor Inn, the museum is open Monday through Friday, 8:00 a.m. to 5:00 p.m. Donations are welcome.

Hubbell Trading Post National Historic Site—John Lorenzo Hubbell, the New Mexico–born son of a U.S. soldier, founded this trading post in 1878. It became the center of his Navajo Reservation trade empire, which grew to include 24 trading posts as well as stage and freight lines. Arriving among the Navajo soon after the second Long Walk, as the people were struggling to adjust to reservation life, Hubbell served as the Indians' spokesman and contact with the white world for over 50 years. He wrote, "The first duty of an Indian trader is to advise them to produce that which their natural inclinations and talent best adapts them, to find a market for their products and vigilantly watch that they keep improving in the production of same, and advise them which commands the best price." Hubbell encouraged the Navajo to develop the high-quality rug weaving and silversmithing for which they are known today.

Hubbell Trading Post, the oldest continuously active trading post on the reservation, still sells food and dry goods to the Indians and excellent-quality Navajo goods to tourists. Weavers and silversmiths demonstrate their arts at the visitors center. Take a free guided tour of Hubbell's home and grounds. Both the trading post and the visitors center are open daily from 8:00 a.m. to 6:00 p.m. in the summer, 8:00 a.m. to 5:00 p.m. the rest of the year. Admission is free.

Canyon de Chelly National Monument—Taking the north rim drive this evening and seeing the south rim (Canyon del Muerto) tomorrow morning will let you make the most of the fairly limited automobile sightseeing possibilities at Canyon de Chelly National Monument. The overlooks along the two scenic drives afford the only views you get of Canyon de Chelly and Canyon del Muerto unless you take a horseback trip into the canyon with a Navajo guide. Traditional Navajo herdsmen live in hogans below the sheer, impassable cliffs, seemingly oblivious to the tourists who daily peer down at them from the rim. To explore the canyon, use binoculars.

Canyon de Chelly (the name, pronounced "d'SHAY," is an Anglo mispronunciation of a Spanish misspelling of Tsegi, Navajo for "rock canyon") is the traditional center of the Navajo lands. According to their mythology, the Navajo people and animals emerged into the world from this place.

Canyon de Chelly National Monument headquarters area has a visitors center (open daily, 8:00 a.m. to 6:00 p.m. May through September, 8:00 a.m. to 5:00 p.m. October through April), campground, and lodge. There is no admission fee to Canyon de Chelly. Various brochures available at the visitors center cost 50 cents each.

Take the 22-mile (each way) scenic drive from the visitors center along the south rim of **Canyon de Chelly**. Tsegi Overlook, 2½ miles along the road, affords an excellent view of traditional hogans and farms on the canyon floor, and 1.4 miles beyond that is Junction Overlook, where you can see two early Anasazi ruins. Two miles farther on is White House Overlook; about 150 yards to the right of the overlook is the only nonguided hiking trail into Canyon de Chelly, a 2-hour, 2½-mile round-trip, 500-foot descent to the large White House Ruin. Bring water. Fifteen miles from there, at the upper end of the canyon, is the overlook for Spider Rock, a solitary 800-foot pinnacle on top of which, according to legend, Spider Woman lives. Not a comic book character, Spider Woman is the mythological being who taught Navajo women the art of weaving. Spider Rock is the last stop on the south rim scenic drive. Return to the visitors center the same way you came.

Tribal Road 64 goes from the park headquarters area to the small Navajo college town of Tsaile, 35 miles away, but sightseers need only drive the first 18 miles to see all the view points along the north rim of **Canyon del Muerto**, then return by the same route. Five miles up the road from the visitors center is Ledge Ruin Viewpoint, an unexcavated Anasazi ruin that had about 50 rooms and two kivas. Three miles farther up the road is Antelope House Overlook, named for the paintings of antelope on the canyon wall to the left of the ruin, probably painted by a Navajo artist in the early 19th century. Nearby paintings of hands and other figures are from the Anasazi people who lived here as early as the 7th century.

Ten more miles up the road will bring you to a turnoff on your right (south) to Mummy Cave and Massacre Cave overlooks. Mummy Cave is the site of one of the largest Anasazi ruins in the canyon, a 77-room, Mesa Verde-style cliff dwelling with a three-story tower. Discovery in the 1880s of two mummies buried at this site gave the canyon its name (which means "Canyon of the Dead"). Massacre Cave was so named because a Spanish expedition slaughtered 115 Indians here in 1805.

Lodging

Rooms at Canyon de Chelly's **Thunderbird Lodge**, near the visitors center and campground, (928) 674-5841, start around $100 double ($35 less off-season). **Best Western Canyon de Chelly Inn**, (928) 674-5875, 1½ miles away on the outskirts of Chinle, has rooms in the same price range. So does the **Holiday Inn** in Chinle, (928) 674-5000.

Food

The cafeteria at **Thunderbird Lodge**, open 7:00 a.m. to 8:30 p.m., serves good food at moderate prices. Try a Navajo taco—Indian-style fry bread heaped with meat, beans, lettuce, and cheese. Although $6 might sound like a high price for a taco, this one will fill you up with some left over. Navajo sand paintings displayed in the cafeteria are among the finest you'll see anywhere.

Nearby, Chinle has a shopping center with a Basho's supermarket and a pizza place, as well as two local cafés.

Camping

Canyon de Chelly's **Cottonwood Campground,** half a mile from the visitors center, has rest rooms, picnic tables, water, and a dumping station but no hookups or showers. Camping is free. Rangers present campfire programs nightly during the summer months.

Hiking and Horseback Trips

Visitors are allowed down into Canyon de Chelly or Canyon del Muerto only when accompanied by Navajo guides, to protect the ancient ruins, the present-day residents' privacy, and you (from quicksand and flash floods), but you can arrange guided tours. The most exciting option is a one-day horseback trip up-canyon to Mummy Cave or Antelope House. For information and reservations, inquire at the visitors center. Half-day or all-day four-wheel-drive tours can be arranged at Thunderbird Lodge. Navajo guides to accompany you up-canyon on a hike or in your own four-wheel-drive vehicle can be arranged through Tsegi Guide Association at the visitors center.

Helpful Hints

Tourist brochures warn that traditional Navajo may refuse to talk to non-Indian tourists, but my experience has been that most people on the reservation are quite willing to talk with outsiders. What may seem like shyness or unfriendliness is actually cultural difference: Navajo people are taught from childhood not to talk too much, be loud, or start conversations with strangers, and eye contact while speaking is considered impolite. A good way to meet an

Indian who doesn't work in the tourist trade is to offer one a ride. It's safe (but use discretion on the highway from Gallup to Window Rock). Hitching rides is common on the reservation, because there is no public transportation.

While a few older people on the reservation speak no English, nearly all Navajo, young and old alike, are bilingual. Despite early attempts by the U.S. government to eradicate it through boarding school education, the Navajo language is now a source of patriotic and tribal pride thanks largely to the "Code-talkers," 1,500 Navajo men who broadcast secret military messages among Pacific islands during World War II. Navajo was the only American "code" the Japanese never succeeded in deciphering. Listen to spoken Navajo as you drive across the reservation. Several area radio stations have Navajo-language programming at different times throughout the day. Try KTNN Window Rock, 660 on your AM radio dial.

Free camping or driving on back roads is not allowed on the Navajo Reservation unless you obtain a permit from the tribal headquarters in Window Rock first. Any time you leave the pavement, you're trespassing on somebody's grazing land, and back roads are usually somebody's driveway. Back roads on the reservation are often in bad condition, easy to get stuck or lost on. Never enter a hogan or other home uninvited. If you need help, observe Navajo tradition and stop at least 50 yards away, call, then wait until someone comes out to see what you want. Respect for privacy helps ensure that the tribe will continue to welcome visitors.

Two major Native American events take place in the Gallup/Window Rock area in the late summer, and either is worth planning your trip around. The Inter-Tribal Ceremonial and Rodeo, the largest Indian powwow in the nation, takes place Thursday through Sunday the second weekend in August at Red Rocks State Park near Gallup; call (505) 863-3896 for complete information. The Navajo Nation Fair, the Navajo equivalent of a state fair with contest dancing, a rodeo, concerts, carnival rides, and a large, fascinating arts and crafts pavilion, is held Thursday through Sunday of the week following Labor Day. Since it is held on the same weekend as Santa Fe's much better known Fiesta, hardly any non-Indian tourists are among the 80,000 people who visit the Navajo Nation Fair each year.

Monument Valley

For a close-up look at traditional Navajo life, drive from Canyon de Chelly in the heart of the Navajo Nation toward the reservation's northern boundary on the edge of Utah's uninhabited slickrock country and visit Monument Valley Tribal Park.

Suggested Schedule

8:00 a.m.	Breakfast
9:00 a.m.	Canyon de Chelly south rim drive.
10:30 a.m.	Drive to Kayenta.
11:30 a.m.	Drive to Navajo National Monument. Picnic and see Betatakin ruins.
2:00 p.m.	Drive to Monument Valley.
3:30 p.m.	Explore Monument Valley.
5:00 p.m.	Camp at Monument Valley or stay at Goulding's Trading Post.

Travel Route: Chinle to Monument Valley (104 miles)

Leaving Canyon de Chelly, take US 191 north from Chinle for 15 miles to the barely noticeable community of Many

Farms, and turn left (west) there on Tribal Route 59. A 58-mile drive along the base of Black Mesa will bring you to US 160. Turn left (west again) and go 8 miles to Kayenta. To visit Navajo National Monument, continue west on US 160 for 22 miles, then go 9 miles north on AZ 564. After visiting Navajo National Monument, retrace your route back to Kayenta. From Kayenta to Monument Valley is 23 miles via US 163.

Sightseeing Highlights

Navajo National Monument—The monument protects major cliff dwellings of the Kayenta culture, the third major Anasazi group (the others being the Chaco and Mesa Verde cultures). The only easily accessible ruin is Betatakin, which can be seen from the easy 1-mile trail that starts at the visitors center. If you have extra time, consider a guided 16-mile wilderness hike or horseback trip into the backcountry to see Keet Seel, the largest cliff dwelling in Arizona and one of the best preserved anywhere. Keet Seel was occupied for only 25 years, yet centuries later, charcoal remains in the hearths, and there are dried ears of corn in the grain storage rooms. For information and reservations, contact Navajo National Monument, H.C. 63, Box 3, Tonalea, AZ 86044, (928) 672-2366.The number of visitors to Keet Seel is limited to 25 per day, so make reservations well in advance.

Monument Valley Navajo Tribal Park—A combination of strange landscape, traditional Navajo life, and sincere if humble tribal hospitality gives the valley a special quality that is unrivaled. As you overlook Monument Valley from the visitors center, you may be struck by déjà vu. This desert landscape, with its spirelike buttes and mesas, has been background scenery for so many Western movies, TV shows, and commercials that you'll recognize it instantly. John Ford's Point is named after the director of *Stagecoach* (1938), the first of many motion pictures filmed here.

Taking the 17-mile unpaved road through the valley seems like driving through a movie, too. Along the way you'll discover the real magic of Monument Valley. This is not an open-air folk museum, and the people have not been hired to look picturesque for tourists. Their families happened to live here when Monument Valley became a tribal park in 1958, and they still do. Of approximately 100 Navajo who make their homes in Monument Valley, most are descendants of families who fled here a century ago to escape the Long Walk.

A guided tour is worthwhile in Monument Valley, since some roads are for four-wheel-drive tour vehicles only. Of several tours available at the visitors center, I recommend Navajo Guided Tour Service, the only company whose owner-operators were born and raised in Monument Valley. All of their tours cover the same 28-mile backcountry route, including Anasazi ruins, petroglyphs, and a visit to the guide's grandmother's hogan. Longer trips proceed at a slower pace. Sunrise and sunset trips cost slightly more. Monument Valley's visitors center and scenic drive are open from 7:00 a.m. to 8:00 p.m. May through September, 8:00 a.m. to 5:00 p.m. October through April. Admission is $3 per person, free for children under 8.

Lodging and Food

Goulding's Trading Post and Lodge, (435) 727-3231, is in the opposite direction from the Monument Valley entrance gate, 2 miles west of US 163. The historic trading post has been operated by the same family for almost 70 years. Rooms run $109 a night and up during tourist season, as low as $68 off-season. Goulding's also has a grocery store, a service station, a restaurant, and good-quality Navajo handicrafts.

Camping

Monument Valley has a 100-site campground. The camp-sites are small and close together, but there is boundless open space for evening desert walking nearby. Best of all, the central rest rooms have pay showers.

Hiking and Biking

At Navajo National Monument, a guided 16-mile wilderness hike or horseback trip will take you through cedar-studded red rock backcountry to **Keet Seel**, Arizona's largest cliff dwelling. For information and reservations, contact Navajo National Monument. Unlike Canyon de Chelly, the daily number of visitors allowed to take the Keet Seel tour is quite limited, so make reservations well in advance by contacting the park administration at the address or phone listed above under Sightseeing Highlights.

Trail of the Ancients to Moab

Today begins a four-day adventure across southern Utah. The journey will take you through some of the most magnificent scenery in the Southwest, including four national parks and the nation's largest national monument. It won't take you through many towns, though. Moab, with a population of 4,000, is the region's largest community.

Today you'll follow the Trail of the Ancients north to Moab. Camp tonight on the Island in the Sky in the center of Canyonlands National Park and explore Arches National Park tomorrow morning.

Moab was a boomtown in the 1950s, when uranium prospecting along the Colorado River was big business. While other uranium towns have practically vanished from the map, Moab has flourished as a tourist town thanks to two national parks nearby, Arches and Canyonlands. This is the place to fill up on gas and stock up on food and water.

Suggested Schedule

8:00 a.m.   Drive to Natural Bridges National Monument.

9:30 a.m.   Natural Bridges scenic drive and hike.

11:30 a.m. Drive to Blanding.

12:30 p.m. Picnic at Devil's Canyon.

1:30 p.m.   Drive on to Moab.

4:00 p.m.   Arrive in Moab, continue to Canyonlands Island in the Sky District.

5:00 p.m.   Explore Island in the Sky. Camp at Canyonlands or Dead Horse Point, or spend the night in Moab.

Travel Route: Monument Valley to Natural Bridges (64 miles)

From Monument Valley, go northeast on US 163 for 26 miles, passing through the small town of Mexican Hat, Utah, on the Navajo Reservation boundary line. Just north of town on your right you'll see the town's namesake—a rock formation that looks like an upside-down sombrero. Soon after you pass the hat, turn left (west) on UT 261, known as the Trail of the Ancients.

Two scenic overlooks on the San Juan River, each a short drive from the highway, deserve a look, especially if you're recording your trip with photographs. Goosenecks State Reserve (three-quarters of a mile from where you turned onto UT 261, left 4 miles on a paved road, $3 entrance fee) affords a close-up view of 1,500-foot-deep entrenched river meanders. Six miles farther north, a 4-mile unpaved road on your left goes to Muley Point, with a broader view of the river's labyrinth and an interpretive display on the area's geology; free, no facilities. Twenty-four miles north on UT 261 from the Muley Point turnoff, you'll come to UT 95. Turn left (west), and in less than a mile you'll reach the turnoff on your right to Natural Bridges.

Natural Bridges National Monument

Tour Natural Bridges National Monument on the paved 8-mile scenic loop drive. The three natural bridges are located in two adjacent canyons, with a hiking trail to each one from the scenic loop. Owachomo Bridge is an easy half-mile hike, while Sipapu and Kachina bridges are each reached by a steep 1½-mile trail. Afternoon temperatures in the summer often reach 100 degrees, so if you'd like to hike either of the longer trails, start early and plan to complete your hike before noon. The monument also has Anasazi cliff dwellings and pictographs. The visitors center (open 8:00 a.m. to 4:30 p.m.) relies entirely on solar electricity. In 1980, when it was built, it was the largest photovoltaic system on earth. Admission to the monument is $6 per vehicle.

Travel Route: Natural Bridges to Moab (108 miles)

Drive east from Natural Bridges on UT 95 a distance of 32 miles to Blanding. Along the way, a well-marked half-mile dirt road to the right (south) goes to **Cave Towers**, seven Anasazi fortress towers used in the 11th and 12fth centuries to defend a permanent underground spring in a cave below. If you are driving a low-clearance vehicle, the best plan for seeing this ruin is to park near the highway and walk up the dirt road, about an hour round-trip. There is also a short hiking trail to Indian ruins from the Butler Wash rest area. The easy 1-mile, half-hour round-trip trail goes to an overlook from which numerous ruins can be seen. Join US 191 northbound (left) into Blanding. Just south of town, 2⅓ miles from the junction, a paved access road on the left goes to Westwater Ruin, yet another cliff dwelling. If you dare, cross Westwater Canyon on the swinging bridge to see a small natural bridge.

In Blanding, **Edge of the Cedars State Historical Monument** has a group of small pueblos and kivas, some dating back to 700. The ruins themselves are not outstanding, but the museum is. Open 9:00 a.m. to 6:00 p.m. during the summer months, until 5:00 p.m. the rest of the year. Admission is $5 per vehicle.

Continue north from Blanding on US 191. Four miles north is **Devil's Canyon Campground**, a good picnic stop. Drive all the way to the end of the campground, where you'll find a short (400 yard) trail to the rim of a canyon that thwarted pioneers and road builders for generations.

It's 21 miles from Blanding to the town of Monticello, 55 more miles to Moab, all scenic. Fifteen miles before Moab, on the right, is the improbable **Hole 'n the Rock Home**, a 5,000-square-foot dwelling carved into the red sandstone cliff by the late Albert and Gladys Christensen between 1945 and 1957, still run by their family as a gift and rock shop. If the stone bust of Franklin D. Roosevelt that Albert carved into the cliff face intrigues you, tour the home and see 14 rooms arranged around large pillars. The fireplace has a 65-foot chimney drilled through solid rock. Open 9:00 a.m. to 6:00 p.m. during the summer months, until 5:00 p.m. the rest of the year. Admission is $4 for adults, $2 for children ages 6 to 12.

Sightseeing Highlights

Canyonlands National Park: Island in the Sky—The turnoff to Island in the Sky is to the left off US 191, about 11 miles northwest of Moab, 6 miles past the Arches National Park turnoff. It's 22 miles from the highway to the park entrance. Stop and check in at the ranger station/visitors center, just

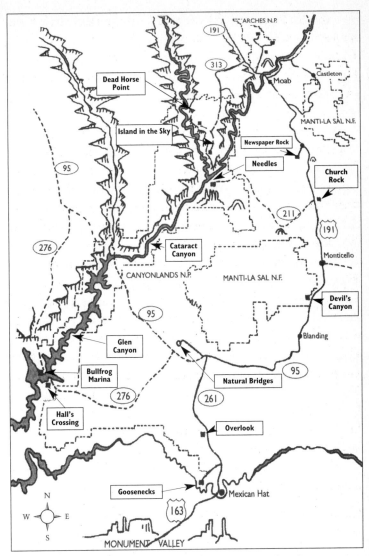

Trail of the Ancients and Canyonlands

past the Neck, a ridge no wider than the road, which is the only way on or off the "island."

Stewart Udall, President Kennedy's Secretary of the Interior, was surveying the site of a proposed dam on the Colorado River above Cataract Canyon from a small plane when he exclaimed, "My God, that's a national park down there!" Two years later, in 1964, Canyonlands National Park became a reality. If your idea of a national park is the Grand Canyon, Yellowstone, or Yosemite, the visitors center (in a converted mobile home) should tip you off that Canyonlands is different. Its 337,570 acres, sliced in thirds by the confluence of the Colorado and Green rivers, contain some of the least accessible land anywhere. Most can only be reached by horseback, raft, or four-wheel drive; some can't be reached at all.

Island in the Sky is a long, narrow promontory between the two rivers, rising 2,000 feet above them. The recently paved roads fork at Green River Overlook, 7 miles past the entrance, and go to opposite ends of the 12-mile-long "island." At the south tip, Grandview Point affords a "look but don't touch" view from the exact center of Canyonlands National Park. Explore with binoculars and let your imagination roam over the marvelously complex landscape.

The White Rim is 1,000 feet below, midway down to river level. Look carefully and you may spot desert bighorn sheep grazing there. A four-wheel-drive road, the Shafer Trail, follows the White Rim all the way around the Island in the Sky. Almost due east is Monument Basin, with its white-capped red-rock fins and spires. In the distance to the east (left) of the Colorado River is the Needles District, where most of the park's long-distance wilderness hiking trails are located. On the opposite side of the Green River, to the southwest, is the Maze. The far rim of the Maze is accessible only by an 80-mile four-wheel-drive road; in The Maze itself there are no developed trails. South as far as you can see, beyond the river junction, the Colorado disappears into Cataract Canyon, which many river-rafters and kayakers consider the ultimate challenge in North America. A member of John Wesley Powell's 1869 Colorado River exploration team likened a boat trip down Cataract Canyon to riding "on the back of the dragon." Beyond Cataract Canyon is an area known simply as Ernie's Country. No road goes there.

Admission to all units of Canyonlands National Park, good for seven days, is $10 per vehicle.

LaSal Mountain Loop—During July and August, early afternoon in both Arches and Canyonlands is likely to be very hot. It's best to drive out to Canyonlands late in the afternoon, when you won't have to wait long for evening's coolness. In the meantime, you might drive the 60-mile LaSal Mountain Loop into cool mountain forests. Go north from Moab on US 191 and turn right onto UT 128 just before the bridge. Follow the Colorado River along the boundary of Arches National Park for 16 miles and take the turnoff to Castle Valley. Go south through Castle Valley 11 miles to the LaSal Mountain Loop Road turnoff on your right, which takes you into the national forest. The loop road will eventually bring you back to US 191 south of Moab. All but one mile of the route is paved.

If you are visiting the area during the cooler fall or spring months, skip the mountains and spend the afternoon seeing Arches National Park or arrive earlier at Canyonlands.

Dan O'Laurie Moab Museum—Located at 118 E. Center Street, this small museum features geological samples and dinosaur fossils to help you comprehend the area's complex landscapes. There are also Indian artifacts from the days when the Ute people lived around Moab and relics of Spanish and United States explorations in the area, as well as pioneer antiques. Open Monday through Saturday from 1:00 to 4:00 p.m. and 7:00 to 9:00 p.m. during the summer months, with more limited hours off-season. Donations are welcome.

Lodging

Moab has a good selection of moderately priced accommodations. Chain motels includes the **Best Western Greenwell Inn**, 105 South Main Street, (435) 259-6151, $45 and up in summer, as low as $39 off-season; the **Ramada Inn**, 182 South Main Street, (435) 259-7141, $55 in summer, as low as $35 off-season; and the **Days Inn**, 426 North Main Street, (435) 259-4468, $86 and up in summer, as low as $43 off-season. Independent motels include the **Inca Inn Motel**, 570 North Main Street, (435) 259-2761, with rooms starting at $46 in the summer, $38 off-season, and the **Red Rock Lodge**, 51 North 100 Street West, (435) 259-5431, $59 and up.

Cedar Breaks Condos, Center and Fourth Street East, (435) 259-7830, offers deluxe lodging in individual condos with kitchens, living rooms, and separate bedrooms, full breakfast included, for $90 double.

Moab's bed and breakfasts are small, so reservations should be made in advance. For deluxe accommodations, try the **Mayor's House Bed & Breakfast Inn**, 505 Rose Tree

Lane, (435) 259-6015, $90 and up. The **Desert Hills Bed & Breakfast**, 1989 Desert Hills Lane, (435) 259-3568, has guest rooms starting at $75 in summer, as low as $50 off-season.

Low-budget accommodations can be found at the Lazy Lizard, an independent hostel located 1 mile south of town behind A-1 Storage. Double rooms cost about $20. Facilities include a kitchen, laundry room, and hot tub. Phone (435) 259-6057.

Food

Moab is the place to stock up on groceries. There are three downtown supermarkets; you won't see another one until you reach Kanab, Utah, three days from now.

The **Bar M Chuckwagon Supper** operates from June through September. Located on the bank of Mill Creek, on the south edge of town off 400 East Street, this ranch-style open-air restaurant serves barbecued beef chuckwagon style, followed by real cowboys singing old-time songs just like in a Roy Rogers movie. The cost is $19.50 for adults, $9.50 for children ages 4 to 10. Call (435) 259-2276 for dinner and show times.

Honest Ozzie's Cafe, 60 North 100 West Street, (435) 259-8442, serves the best vegetarian food in southern Utah as well as tempting, all-natural, not-quite-vegetarian dishes. Look for pastries, gourmet coffee and full breakfasts at **Breakfast at Tiffany's**, 90 East Center Street, (435) 259-2553.

The **Grand Old Ranch House**, 1266 Highway 191 North, (435) 259-5753, serves dinner only (5:00-10:30 p.m. daily) in a turn-of-the-century farmhouse on the

National Register of Historic Places. German cuisine is a specialty.

Moab's finest dining is to be found at the **Sunset Grill**, 900 Highway 191 North, (435) 259-5271. whose modest-sounding name belies the elegant setting in the hilltop former mansion of a uranium mining mogul. The menu features French and Cajun cuisine and seafood.

Camping

Canyonlands National Park's primitive 12-site **Yellow Flat Campground** is near Green River Overlook, 7 miles in from the visitors center. There are rest rooms but no water. The campground may be full by 5:00 p.m., even earlier in spring and fall.

If the campground at Island in the Sky is full when you arrive, go back outside the park boundary to the 7-mile paved side road to **Dead Horse Point State Park**, where you'll find a campground with all facilities and well-developed rim trails overlooking the Colorado River Canyon. This campground is larger and costs more than the one at Canyonlands, so it fills up later.

Another alternative is to spend the night at Arches National Park (see Day 18) and hike the Devil's Garden in the hours before dark or after dawn.

Hiking and Biking

There are few developed hiking trails in the Island in the Sky district of Canyonlands. The best hiking is in the area of Upheaval Dome, the crater of a collapsed salt dome. Two easy trails, each a 1-mile, half-hour walk, leave from the Dome Road near the Picnic area. **Upheaval Dome Trail** goes to the rim of the dome, with views into the center of the crater. **White Rock Trail** takes you to the top of a butte to view the dome from a distance. You can enjoy a longer hike along the canyonlands rim from any of the overlooks, following the unofficial tracks of past hikers. Stay on the bare slickrock surfaces, away from fragile vegetation (and rattlesnakes).

The Moab area has become a mountain bikers' mecca. In the spring and fall months, off-road cycling enthusiasts come by the thousands to ride in and around Canyonlands. Tour companies including **Rim Tours,** 1233 Highway 191 South, (435) 259-5223; **Kaibab Adventure Outfitters,** 391 South Main Street, (435) 259-7423; **Western Spirit Cycling,** 478 Mill Creek Drive, (435) 259-8732; **Dreamriders Mountainbike Tours,** 600 North Main Street, (435) 259-6419; and **Nichols Expeditions,** 497 North Main Street (435) 259-3999), offer guided tours of the canyon country. Day trips cost around $50 per person, and four-day trips along the 100-mile White Rim Trail into the heart of Canyonlands cost about $400 per person. All of these tour outfitters also rent out mountain bikes for individual riding at around $25 a day. Without a tour, you can ride the **Moab Slickrock Bike Trail,** which starts about 2 miles outside town on Sand Flats Road past the city dump. The challenging 10-mile loop trail crosses spectacular undulating expanses of bare rock as it follows an often-steep, winding, sometimes edgy route originally established by off-road motorcyclists but now taken over by bicycles. The trail passes magnificent viewpoints along Negro Bill Canyon and Swiss Cheese Ridge.

Bookstores

Except for National Park visitors centers, Moab has just about the only booksellers in southern Utah:

Back of Beyond Bookstore, 83 North Main, (435) 259-5154.

Canyonlands Natural History Association, 3031 Highway 191 South, (435) 259-6003.

Arches to Capitol Reef

Today holds what may be a once-in-a-lifetime experience: three national parks in the same day. Awaken in Canyonlands and get an early start to tour Arches. Drive during the middle of the day, with a possible stop at Goblin Valley if the weather isn't too hot, and arrive at Capitol Reef in time to enjoy the cool of the evening in the least known of Utah's national parks.

Suggested Schedule

7:30 a.m.	Get an early start, grab a cup of coffee, and drive to Arches National Park.
8:00 a.m.	Hike in Arches during the cool morning hours.
Noon	Drive to Green River for lunch.
1:30 p.m.	Drive to Goblin Valley.
2:30 p.m.	See Goblin Valley.
3:30 p.m.	Drive to Capitol Reef. Camp there or spend the night in nearby Torrey.

Arches National Park

Arches is almost adjacent to Canyonlands. To get there, retrace your route from Island in the Sky to US 191 and go 6 miles east (back toward Moab) to the Arches National Park entrance. Park admission is $10 per vehicle.

Readers of *Desert Solitaire*, the late Edward Abbey's memoir of a season as a ranger in the small, almost inaccessible Arches National Monument in the 1950s, will recall his tirade against "national parkification" and, understandably, brace themselves for a bad case of too many tourists. In reality, it's not that bad. There is traffic on the park's paved roads, and the park service has put up signs telling you the names of all the major rock formations, but it's hardly Disneyland. Arrive as early in the morning as possible to beat both the heat and the press of other tourists.

Arches National Park, more than half of which is bare rock, centers around a collapsed salt dome similar to Canyonlands' Upheaval Dome but larger. Salt deposits from ancient seas floated up to form a large underground deposit that fractured surface layers of sandstone, then groundwater dissolved the salt and washed it away. The dome collapsed, leaving a rim of fin formations, which freezing and thawing carved to make natural arches. The park has more natural arches than any other place in the world.

Travel Route: Arches to Capitol Reef (171 miles)

From the Arches National Park entrance, turn right (northwest) on US 191 and go 26 miles to Crescent Junction. Take I 70 westbound for 20 miles to Green River. Green River State Park, on the outskirts of town, has expansive green lawns and shade trees, a cool and pleasant picnic spot that could be worth the $3/day use fee.

Eleven miles west of Green River, exit the interstate southbound on UT 24 to Hanksville, a distance of 51 miles. At 30 miles, you'll see a large sign on the right to **Goblin Valley State Park**. If you have time, take the 11-mile (last 6 unpaved) road into the park. There is a $2/day use fee. Goblin Valley's weird rock formations are unlike any other weird rock formations you've seen: Imagine giant petrified milk chocolate–covered Walt Disney mushrooms, set against a backdrop of buttes eroded to resemble Mayan pyramids. If you can imagine that, you'll love this place. It may be too hot to walk through the valley in midafternoon. If you'd like to spend the night here and see it in the early evening but don't want to pay the camping fee (there's no water anyway), camp free around the other side of the butte on the Wild Horse Butte road, which branches off just before the park entrance.

From Hanksville, continuing on UT 24, it's 30 miles to the entrance of Capitol Reef National Park.

Capitol Reef National Park

Capitol Reef may be the national park system's best-kept secret. Established in 1971, it remains the least visited of Utah's national parks. Besides offering a variety of short and long hiking trails, unpaved auto roads, four-wheel-drive roads, and trackless wilderness, the park protects ancient petroglyphs, a well-preserved Mormon pioneer village, and orchards where visitors can pick fruit right off the trees. Admission to the park is $4 per vehicle.

The park's most visible points of interest, listed in order

below, cluster along UT 24 on the nine-mile drive up the Fremont River from the entrance gate to the visitors center and campground. Take your time. Tomorrow morning you'll have a chance to sample the park's backcountry.

Capitol Reef Sightseeing Highlights

Behunin Cabin—Elijah Behunin, the area's first settler (1882), lived with his wife and ten children in this stone cabin, which was smaller than most modern camping vehicles. The next time you have to huddle in your rig or tent until the rain stops, think of Elijah.

Hickman Bridge—A one-mile (each way) trail climbs switchbacks 380 feet through a small canyon and under the 133-foot natural bridge. Along the way are Indian ruins and fine views of white-capped domes, including Capitol Dome, for which the "reef" (uplifted cliff) is named. Allow two hours for the hike.

Petroglyphs—Fremont Indians, who lived here at least as early as 800, left this rock art for us to admire. Experts do not know its meaning; do you? The best petroglyphs are reached on a short, easy trail from the parking pullout.

Fruita Schoolhouse—This country school served the pioneer community of Fruita (originally named "The Eden of Wayne County"), where the visitors center and campground are now located. The school, used from 1896 to 1941, is the only building left standing.

Orchards—While no houses remain from old Fruita, the 2,500 cherry, apple, peach, and apricot trees that were the village's lifeblood endure, preserved by the National Park Service as a Historic Landscape. Pruning, irrigation, and replanting are done by park service employees. When

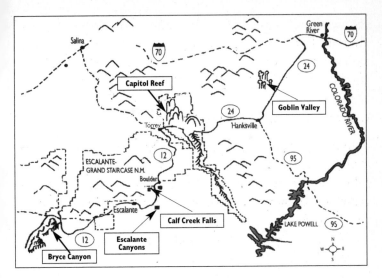

Capitol Reef to Bryce Canyon

the fruit ripens, the public is invited to pick it, then pay the park service the same price per pound that local orchards get. Harvest dates are posted at the visitors center.

Fremont River Trail—An easy walk upriver from the campground through the orchards will bring you to the trail, which follows the riverbank for half a mile. If you're feeling adventurous and have at least 2½ hours, stay on the trail for the steep climb—800 feet in three-quarters of a mile—up Miner's Peak for a fine view of Fruita and the reef.

Lodging and Food

Capitol Reef National Park has no lodge or restaurant, but the **Best Western Capitol Reef Resort**, (435) 425-3761, $99 and up in summer, as low as $59 off-season, is located just a mile outside the park's west entrance. Three miles from the west entrance, the antique-filled **Sky Ridge Bed & Breakfast Inn,** (435) 425-3222, offers luxury accommodations starting at $107. In the same area, the **Wonderland Inn and Restaurant,** (435) 425-3775, has hilltop accommodations starting at $58 in summer, $40 off-season, and a dining room with a spectacular view. You'll find plenty of other motels and a few bed and breakfasts, as well as restaurants and service stations, in the town of Torrey, 11 miles west of the visitors center on US 12. For a unique experience, try the **Cockscomb Inn,** State Road 3262, (435) 425-3511, a bed and breakfast in a circa 1900 polygamist farmhouse; rooms start at $60.

Camping

Fruita Campground at Capitol Reef National Park is the only federal campground in the Southwest with a green lawn at each campsite. It is on the riverbank, surrounded by orchards, with two trails for evening or morning walks. Nightly naturalist slide shows are presented at the campground amphitheater from May through September.

If you're traveling in July or August, and you arrive after 6:00 p.m., you may find the Capitol Reef campground full. There are three national forest campgrounds higher in the mountains, within 20 miles southeast of Torrey on UT 12. The first, **Singletree,** offers a good view of the valley and beyond to the Henry Mountains, the last place in the lower 48 United States to be explored and mapped. **Pleasant Creek** and neighboring **Oak Creek campgrounds** are said to have marauding skunks ("Thousands of skunks!" according to the campground host). Stash all food inside your vehicle at night.

Hiking and Biking

Arches National Park is hiking country, with ten outstanding trails. The hike that will show you the most in a short visit is the **Devil's Garden Trail** from the campground at the end of the 21-mile main road. This moderate 5-mile loop trail leads to seven arches, including Landscape Arch, the world's longest natural span. It is the most popular trail in the park. For more remote hiking, turn off the main road onto the unpaved road to Wolfe Ranch. At the old ranch cabin, you'll find the trailhead for **Delicate Arch Trail**, a steep 3-mile round-trip to perhaps the park's most beautiful arch. Allow from three to four hours for either hike.

Starting just across the road from the campground at Capitol Reef, the **Cohab Canyon Trail** climbs a quarter-mile by switchbacks to a slickrock canyon, goes almost 2 miles through the canyon, and comes out at the river across the road from the Hickman Bridge trailhead. (Cohab Canyon and Hickman Bridge trails can be combined for a great all-morning hike.) The canyon got its name because, so the story goes, Mormon "cohabitationists" used it to hide out from U.S. marshals trying to enforce the federal law against polygamy.

Bicyclists in both Arches and Capitol Reef National Parks are restricted to maintained vehicle roads.

Bryce Canyon National Park

The drive from Capitol Reef to Bryce Canyon, through Grand Staircase–Escalante National Monument, is among the most beautiful stretches of road on this tour. Bryce Canyon is congested with tourist traffic, but the scenery is worth braving the masses. Test your crowd-avoiding strategy (which will also work at the Grand Canyon) by taking an easy walk along the canyon rim or a more demanding one down among the hoodoos.

Suggested Schedule

9:00 a.m.	Capitol Reef Scenic Drive or hike.
Noon	Drive to Calf Creek in Grand Staircase–Escalante National Monument.
1:00 p.m.	Picnic.
2:00 p.m.	Drive to Bryce Canyon National Park.
3:00 p.m.	Get campsite or check into the lodge.
3:30 p.m.	See Bryce Canyon by shuttle or hike.

Capitol Reef Scenic Drive

Spend the morning hiking in Capitol Reef or take the 8-mile unpaved Scenic Drive south from the visitors center. Take time to look at the gigantic 3-D relief map in the visitors center first. A self-guided tour brochure, available free at the visitors center, explains the area's geology.

The last 2 miles of the Scenic Drive were once (from 1884 to 1962) part of the main "highway" through south-central Utah. Beyond the end of the Scenic Drive, the old road continues as Capitol Gorge Trail. An easy 2-mile round-trip hike takes you to Indian petroglyphs, a pioneer register, and the Tanks—pockets in the rock which capture rainwater pools, hence the other name for the Capitol Reef formation, Waterpocket Fold. Butch Cassidy, for years a hero in these parts as he robbed from the rich (plundering trains and banks all over the Four Corners region) and shared with the poor (including not only his gang members but also local folks who guarded the secret of his whereabouts), frequently used this route to reach his hideout nearby.

The scenic drive is not a loop. Drive back to the visitors center the same way you came.

Travel Route: Capitol Reef to Bryce Canyon (104 miles)

Drive west from Capitol Reef on UT 24 for 11 miles. As you near the town of Torrey, turn left (south) on UT 12 and stay on that highway all the way to Bryce Canyon National Park. The first 33 miles of the route climb into Dixie National Forest, through ponderosa forest between Boulder Mountain and Impossible Peak, and descend into the town of Boulder, where **Anasazi Indian Village State Park** ($3 per person, maximum $5 per vehicle) is located. The visitors center here also serves as the main information center for Grand Staircase–Escalante National Monument.

From there, the highway descends into the Escalante Canyons area of **Grand Staircase–Escalante National Monument**. The best picnic stop-and-walk is Calf Creek Recreation Area, on your right about a mile before the bottom of the canyon, where a 2-mile trail leads past two Anasazi village ruins to Calf Creek Falls. Beyond the canyons, 18 miles from Boulder, is the town of Escalante. The local attraction is **Escalante Petrified Forest State Park** ($4 per vehicle entrance fee), which also has cliff dwellings. Forty-two more miles across grazing land will bring you to the entrance of Bryce Canyon National Park. Admission to the national park is $5 per vehicle.

Sightseeing Highlights

Grand Staircase–Escalante National Monument—One of President Clinton's greatest legacies was the creation of no fewer than 15 new national monuments. This was the first and most controversial of them. Unlike national parks, a president can declare federal land a national monument without a Congressional vote. Every past president since Theodore Roosevelt, except for Nixon, Reagan, and Bush, has used this power, but none as dramatically as Clinton. Created to block plans for massive coal strip mining, this 1.9-million-acre area is by far the largest U.S. national monument.

Back in the 1930s, conservationists proposed the creation of Escalante National Park. The plan was rejected. If it had passed, it would have protected a vast area of southern Utah in one of the nation's largest parks. Some of the land has been lost under the water of Lake Powell, and other parts became Capitol Reef and Bryce Canyon National Parks. With the creation of Grand Staircase National Monument, virtually all of the proposed Escalante National Park is now protected and open to the public for recreational use.

Highway 12 between Torrey and Panguitch travels through the national monument for a distance of 68 miles. There are few developed facilities and no entrance fee, but overnight backpackers must obtain a $5 permit from the monument information desk in Boulder.

Bryce Canyon National Park—Brace yourself for Bryce Canyon, a victim of its own success. Anytime between Memorial Day and Labor Day, it will be crowded. Bryce Canyon (formerly Utah National Monument) became a national park in 1923, just four years after the Grand Canyon did. Its proximity to the Grand Canyon makes it an ideal stop on loop tours that take in the North Rim, Zion, and Glen Canyon Dam.

Many times more tourists visit Bryce Canyon than Canyonlands, Arches, and Capitol Reef combined. Over the past two decades, the 18-mile paved drive through the park has become so clogged with traffic that the scenic overlook pullouts are about as much fun as a shopping mall parking lot. During the summer months, rangers report, there have been three to four cars at a time for each parking space in the park. To remedy this, a shuttle (the Blue Line) now runs from a boarding area at the park entrance to the visitors center, with two other shuttles heading from there. The Red Line takes you to the lodge and developed scenic overlooks, while the Green Line takes passengers on a two-hour tour of the less-visited south part of the park. Use of the shuttle is voluntary (so far), but it costs $20 to enter the park by car and only $15 by shuttle.

The eroded shale-and-sandstone uplifts of Bryce Canyon are absolutely unique. The park service even invented a new name for the white and bright orange obelisks and spires: "hoodoo," which they define as "a pinnacle, pillar, or odd-shaped rock left standing by the forces of erosion." Bryce Canyon, by the way, was named after Ebenezer Bryce, a homesteader who tried to graze cattle here between 1875 and 1880. Bryce's opinion of the scenery was, "It's a hell of a place to lose a cow."

Lodging

For a roof over your head, you can do no better than a room or cabin at **Bryce Canyon Lodge**, (435) 834-5361, in the park. The rustic elegance is a bargain at $93 to $120 a night. Reservations are a must. Main lodge units have two queen-size beds, full bath, and private porch. The carpeted cabins have fireplaces.

Other accommodations near the park entrance include **Best Western Ruby's Inn**, (435) 834-5341, $95 in season, as low as $46 in winter; **Bryce Canyon Resorts**, 13500 East Highway 12, (435) 834-5351, $85 in summer, $65 off-season, and **Bryce View Lodge**, Highway 63, (435) 834-5180, $55 and up in summer, as low as $44 off-season. All three are stops on the park's Blue Line shuttle route.

Food

Fine dining can be found at the Bryce Canyon Lodge dining room. Groceries are sold at the Camper Store nearby.

Ruby's Inn near the park entrance has a family-style steak-and-seafood restaurant.

Camping

Bryce Canyon has two campgrounds, **North Campground** and **Sunset Campground**. Together they have 204 campsites, with separate loops for RVs and tent campers. By early afternoon, the campsite registration areas will be a traffic jam of campers and motor homes. Stake your claim to a campsite as soon as you arrive in the park and sightsee afterward. Both campgrounds have campfire programs. Pay showers, laundry facilities, pay telephones and groceries are available at the Sunrise Point Camper Store.

Hiking and Biking

To beat the crowds at Bryce Canyon, walk. Few visitors do, though the park has 60 miles of beautifully maintained trails. The most spectacular formations can be seen on the easy **Rim Trail** that runs 6 miles from Fairyland View to Sunset Point, Sunrise Point, and finally Bryce Point. Take part or all of it. The Red Line shuttle service can drop you off and pick you up at any of the overlooks for one-way hikes. More ambitious hikers with at least five hours to spend can get down among the hoodoos on the strenuous 5½-mile **Fairyland Loop Trail**, which also runs between Sunrise Point and Fairyland View, then take the shuttle back or walk back along the Rim Trail for a good view of where they've been.

Off-road biking is not permitted in Bryce Canyon National Park, but adjacent Grand Staircase–Escalante National Monument contains literally hundreds of miles of primitive roads that are ideal for adventurous cyclists. For maps and information, check in at the Anasazi State Park/Grand Staircase–Escalante National Monument Information Desk, 460 North Highway 12, Boulder, (435) 679-8562. A free permit is required for overnight biking or backpacking.

Lake Powell and Lee's Ferry

After a leisurely, slow-to-get-going morning at Bryce Canyon, drive down to the Colorado River. You saw it on Day 17 from Island in the Sky, and you'll see it again tomorrow from the rim of the Grand Canyon. Today, you'll see the river in two of its other aspects: from the top of its largest dam and, just a few miles downriver, from the exact spot where the Grand Canyon begins.

Suggested Schedule

9:00 a.m.	Hike at Bryce Canyon.
10:00 a.m.	Drive from Bryce Canyon to Kanab. Lunch there.
1:30 p.m.	Drive to Glen Canyon Dam.
3:00 p.m.	Take the dam tour.
4:30 p.m.	Drive to Lee's Ferry.
5:30 p.m.	Camp at Lee's Ferry.

Travel Route: Bryce Canyon to Lee's Ferry (126 miles)

Leaving Bryce Canyon, take UT 12 westbound, 13 miles through Red Canyon to the intersection with US 89. From here on, it's impossible to get lost. Just follow the big green-and-white Grand Canyon signs. Turn south (left) on US 89 and stay on it all the way to Kanab, 61 miles. Along the way, watch on your left for the privately operated Moqui Cave. The real attraction is the entrance in the shape of a triceratops—a classic bit of tourist kitsch.

There's a supermarket in Kanab, in case you're low on provisions. From Kanab, stay on US 89 to Lake Powell. The driving distance to Glen Canyon Dam is 85 miles.

After touring the dam, continue south for 23 more miles, across the corner of the Navajo Reservation, to Bitter Springs, where Alternate US 89 turns north (right) to Marble Canyon. Another 14 miles will bring you to Navajo Bridge, the first bridge across the Colorado River when it was built in the 1920s. Just past the village of Marble Canyon, follow the 4-mile road on your right (north) to Lee's Ferry, Glen Canyon National Recreation Area.

Sightseeing Highlights

Glen Canyon Dam (Glen Canyon National Recreation Area)—The northernmost and largest of the dams that form the Colorado River Project (the other major ones are Hoover Dam on Lake Mead, Davis Dam on Lake Mojave, and Parker Dam on Lake Havasu), Glen Canyon Dam generates unimaginable amounts of electricity and sends it by power lines straight across 600 miles of desert to southern California. Take the guided tour into the bowels of the dam to see the water turbines and the long row of transformers, each of which pours out 345,000 volts of electricity.

Environmentalists have never forgiven the government for building this dam, which flooded one of the last unexplored areas in the United States. It may seem strange that, with all this water and energy, the surrounding land is arid and empty. Virtually none of the water in the Colorado River or its reservoirs is used for irrigation until it reaches southern California. About one-third of the river's water evaporates from the lake surfaces. What remains is diverted by pipeline just north of the Mexican border to irrigate the Imperial Valley. Glen Canyon Dam traps Colorado River silt, sand, and mining wastes, filling up the lakebed several feet each year. In less than two centuries, experts say, Lake Powell will be a vast barren mud flat, while the dam, its generators rusted and silent, will be one of the world's largest man-made waterfalls. (Powell Falls National Monument? Squint your eyes and you can almost see it.)

The visitors center is open daily from 7:00 a.m. to 7:00 p.m. during the summer months and 8:30 a.m. to 5:30 p.m. the rest of the year. Guided tours of the dam leave frequently from the visitors center and are included in the admission fee, $5 per vehicle. The same fee also covers Lee's Ferry, below the dam.

Change your watch when you cross the dam. Arizona does not change to Daylight Savings Time, as other southwestern states do. Most Arizonans live in the hot climate of Phoenix and Tucson, where they prefer long cool summer evenings, not more daylight. When it's 4:00 p.m. on the Utah side of the dam, it's 3:00 p.m. on the Arizona side.

John Wesley Powell Museum—This museum and area information center at Lake Powell Boulevard and Navajo Drive in Page, about 2 miles past the dam on the Arizona side, recounts the adventures of the man who led the first expedition down the Colorado River through Cataract Canyon and the Grand Canyon (1869), braving the whitewater in wooden boats. There are also Indian artifacts and exhibits that explain the geology of the river and its canyons. The museum is open weekdays from 8:00 a.m. to 6:00 p.m., Tuesday until 8:00 p.m., and Sunday from 10:00 a.m. to 6:00 p.m., closed Saturday, during the summer months; in the spring and October, it closes at 5:00 p.m. and is not open on weekends; closed during the winter months. Admission is $1 for adults, 50¢ for children ages 5 to 13.

Lee's Ferry (Glen Canyon National Recreation Area)— John D. Lee established the first ferry across the Colorado River here in Marble Canyon in 1871. He was a fugitive at the time for leading fellow Mormons to massacre a wagon train of California-bound pioneers. He came here to hide, went into business, and lived here with one of his 17 wives until U.S. marshals found him and shot him.

Lee's Ferry is still the only road to river level on the Colorado between Green River, Utah, and the California state line, a distance of over 600 river miles. Though just a few miles downriver from Glen Canyon Dam, here in Marble Canyon you'll find rare, wild beauty barely touched by mankind. Lee's Ferry is the departure point for all white-water rafting and kayaking expeditions into the Grand Canyon. You can watch them set out any morning from the launch ramp at the end of the road.

On the river, across the main road from the campground, is a long sandy beach, the easiest water access for area wildlife and the only place you're likely to spot a beaver in the desert. Temperatures by the river are much cooler than at the campground. As you bask on the beach, notice the narrow strip of white limestone that rises diagonally out of the water on the cliffs across the river. Here is where the Grand Canyon begins: The white layer keeps slanting upward to become the surface of the Kaibab Plateau, the rim of the Grand Canyon.

Lodging

The small town of Page, on the Arizona side of Glen Canyon Dam, has a handful of brand-name motor inns that cater primarily to boating enthusiasts, such as the **Holiday Inn Express**, 751 South Navajo Drive, (928) 645-9000, $79 and up in summer, as low as $45 off-season, and the **Best Western Arizona Inn**, 716 Rimview Drive, (928) 645-2466, $69 and up in summer, as low as $49 off-season.

There are also several big, resortish places overlooking the lake, such as the 350-room **Wahweap Lodge**, 100 Lakeshore Drive, (928) 645-2433, $150 in summer, $105 off-season.

Look for more rustic lodging at the **Marble Canyon Lodge**, (928) 355-2225, located at the Lee's Ferry turnoff just west of Navajo Bridge. It also has a restaurant, convenience store, service station, and fishing supplies.

Camping

Lee's Ferry Campground has rest rooms, water, and picnic tables with shade roofs. Used primarily by fishermen, the campground is crowded on weekends but practically empty during the week. There are no hookups.

Boating and Hiking

To arrange boat rentals or charters, including houseboats, call Wahweap Marina, (928) 645-2433.

For information on all-day boat excursions from Glen Canyon Dam to **Rainbow Bridge National Monument**, the world's largest known natural bridge (290 feet high and spanning 270 feet), 50 miles northwest, contact the Superintendant, Glen Canyon National Recreation Area, Box 1507, Page, AZ 86040, (928) 608-6404.

It is also possible to hike to the national monument, a rugged 14-mile (one-way) trek from the dam. Since Rainbow Bridge is a sacred place to the Navajo Indians in the area, and the trail crosses Navajo land, hikers must obtain a permit from the Navajo Nation Parks Department, P.O. Box 308, Window Rock, AZ 86515. Camping is not permitted within the monument boundaries.

The Grand Canyon—North Rim

The North Rim of the Grand Canyon is a thousand feet higher than the South Rim—8,255 feet above sea level and about 4,300 feet above the Colorado River in the bottom of the canyon. Some people contend that the view is better from the South Rim, because you can see the river from there. I like the North Rim view just fine, the climate is cooler, and this side of the canyon is less visited and less extensively developed.

Suggested Schedule

8:30 a.m.	Drive to Jacob Lake.
10:00 a.m.	Drive to the North Rim of the Grand Canyon.
Noon	Arrive at the North Rim. Get a campsite or check into the lodge. Lunch.
1:00 p.m.	Relax on a gentle walk along the Transept Trail out to Bright Angel Point, or a longer hike on one of the trails to remote overlooks.
Evening	Dine in or out. Catch the campfire talk or join a night sky walk to Bright Angel Point.

Travel Route: Lee's Ferry to Grand Canyon North Rim (83 miles)

Get an early start. The Grand Canyon North Rim campground often fills up by noon.

A 41-mile drive west on US 89 Alternate will take you up through the ponderosa pine forests of the Kaibab Plateau to Jacob Lake. Turn south on AZ 67. Near the intersection, you'll see a portable park service building by the side of the road. Stop for information on campsite availability at the Grand Canyon. If there is any problem, the rangers will direct you to alternate campgrounds in the national forest. From Jacob Lake, it's 42 more miles on AZ 67 to the North Rim.

The Grand Canyon

Unlike the South Rim, the North Rim has no museums, scenic rim drives, or IMAX theaters to distract visitors from the world's most awe-inspiring scenery. In fact, just about the only thing to do here is hike out to one of the rock points on the rim and admire the view, thinking, "Wow! The Grand Canyon!"

Although the North Rim receives only a fraction of the visitors the South Rim does, facilities are fewer, so it may be hard to find a parking space, let alone a room or campsite.

Admission to the Grand Canyon is $20 per vehicle, valid on both rims of the canyon for 7 days. The North Rim, much higher in elevation than the South Rim, gets so much snow in the winter that it is only open from mid-May through October.

Lodging

Grand Canyon Lodge, (928) 638-2611, the only North

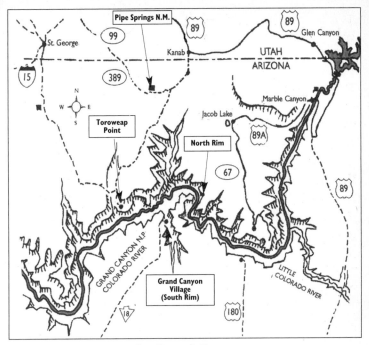

The Grand Canyon

Rim accommodation within the park, offers modern guest rooms as well as three types of individual cabins. Prices range between $75 and $100 double. Make reservations well in advance.

Slightly lower-cost accommodations, with a pleasant forest setting but no canyon view, can be found at **Jacob Lake Inn**, (928) 643-7232. Rates are in the $70 range, slightly higher for cottages.

Food

The dining room at the **Grand Canyon Lodge**, with its panoramic picture window view, serves a limited selection of fine food for breakfast, lunch, and dinner. Reservations are essential for dinner; go to the lodge and make them in person as early in the day as possible. Breakfast overlooking the Grand Canyon is an experience to remember.

Camping

North Rim Campground, perched practically on the edge of the Grand Canyon, has 86 campsites, first-come, first-served. The campground has a laundromat and coin-operated showers. This is not a large campground for such a popular area. In fact, the North Rim has only about one-third the campground capacity of Bryce Canyon. If the campground is full, as it may well be if you arrive later than noon, the rangers at the Jacob Lake information booth will point you toward another campground in the national forest and tell you what time to line up if you want a North Rim campsite tomorrow. To assure a campsite at the rim, you can make reservations (at least a month in advance) by calling Biospherics, (800) 365-2267.

Hiking and Biking

Even at the Grand Canyon, one of the nation's most popular parks, you can find solitude by hiking one of the trails that lead to more isolated points along the rim. Some are longer than others, but all are level and easy to walk.

The popular **Transept Trail** leads 1½ miles from the campground to the lodge along the canyon rim. An extension of the trail from the lodge goes another quarter-mile to Bright Angel Point.

A longer and less-frequented route is the **Uncle Jim Trail,** which starts from the North Kaibab Trailhead. From the campground, cross the main road and follow the path around the water tanks; when you reach the road again, you're there. Follow the trail that goes back into the woods, not the one that goes down into the canyon. It is a 5-mile round-trip walk to Uncle Jim Point (named for Jim Owens, the warden of Grand Canyon Game Preserve until it became a national park in 1919). Allow three hours for the walk.

The **Ken Patrick Trail** branches to the left from Uncle Jim Trail 1 mile along and goes another 10 miles (one way) to Point Imperial. The hike takes six hours each way. It goes deep into the forest but affords canyon views only around Point Imperial, to which you can also drive. The most practical plan for hiking this trail is to drive to Point Imperial and walk partway back along the trail, or arrange for someone less athletic than you to drive out there in six hours and pick you up.

Perhaps the most enjoyable rim walk in the park is the **Widforss Trail**. The trailhead is 1 mile in on a dirt road that leaves the main road 1¼ miles from the campground, one-quarter mile from the Cape Royal Road junction. This 10-mile round-trip (allow five hours) skirts the Transept rim, then takes you into the forest and brings you back to the rim overlooking Haunted Canyon. There is a picnic area at Widforss Point (named for Gunnar Widforss, a Swedish artist who made a career of painting America's national parks in the 1920s).

You can hike partway down the **North Kaibab Trail**, but be warned: The first part of the trail is the steepest, dropping 2,000 feet in not much more than a mile. Climbing back up will take four times as long as going down. An all-day, 9½-mile round-trip hike to the swimming holes near where Roaring Springs Canyon joins Bright

Angel Creek will make you feel like you've hiked the Grand Canyon.

Itinerary Option: Pipe Springs and Grand Canyon–Parashant National Monuments

If solitude is what you crave and a 140-mile drive on unpaved roads doesn't intimidate you, allow an extra day in your itinerary for a drive out to Toroweap Point near the west end of the canyon, where you can be alone on the rim for a more personal Grand Canyon experience.

This area was originally part of Grand Canyon National Monument, created by President Theodore Roosevelt in 1919. Because it was so hard to reach or staff, it was omitted from the act that made the Grand Canyon a national park, leaving its legal status in doubt until 1975, when the national monument was officially abandoned. Then, in 2000, President Clinton declared the former Grand Canyon National Monument, along with a vast area of the Arizona Strip stretching all the way to the Nevada state line, a new national monument named Grand Canyon–Parashant. Like Grand Staircase–Escalante National Monument to the north, Grand Canyon–Parashant National Monument is one of the largest U.S. national monuments, encompassing more than one million acres. The government anticipates no facilities or improvements to this wild landscape except for erecting an information kiosk at Toroweap Point and moving the primitive campground on the point back away from the canyon rim.

This route involves driving on unpaved roads for 67 miles to Toroweap Point today and another 67 (or more) unpaved miles back out tomorrow. The roads are wide and well-graded—better, in fact, than some paved highways you've driven on the Navajo Reservation—but there is no gas, food, or water anywhere. Nobody lives out here. If your vehicle breaks down and you can't fix it, you may have a long wait before anyone comes along and can fetch help, so carry twice as much food and water as you think you'll need. Don't try this trip if thunderstorms threaten; flash floods are possible, and the road can be slippery when wet. Storms occur in the afternoon, almost never in the morning.

From the North Rim, retrace your route to Jacob Lake and Fredonia, a distance of 75 miles. At Fredonia, turn west (left) on AZ 389 and go 15 miles to Pipe Springs National Monument on the Kaibab Paiute Indian Reservation. Around the 9-mile point on the way, watch for the unpaved road that goes south. This is the road you'll want to take after seeing Pipe Springs.

A well-preserved remnant of Mormon pioneer life, the ranch that is now **Pipe Springs National Monument** was established to graze cattle tithed to the church by ranchers throughout the Arizona Strip. The founder's name was Winsor so, naturally enough, the fortresslike stone main house bears the nickname "Winsor Castle." As the only telegraph station in the Strip, the ranch became a communications center. Women from the historical society in Fredonia, wearing authentic period dress, demonstrate weaving, quilting, and other pioneer crafts in the castle's antique-furnished rooms. Open 8:00 a.m. to 5:00 p.m.

The drive to Toroweap Point takes you across the Arizona Strip (no relation to the Las Vegas Strip). Pioneer ranchers discovered the area in the 1870s, at a time when there were several years of exceptional rainfall. Thinking they'd discovered a cattleman's paradise, they moved large beef herds into the area. Then the rain stopped. The cattle overgrazed the sparse vegetation, then starved. Today a handful of Paiute and Anglo ranchers run a few cattle over the vast area, but you're more likely to see pronghorn antelope. The signs on the road to Toroweap are confusing. The inconspicuous sign at the highway turnoff says the road goes to Mt. Trumbull. Follow signs to Tuweap, Toroweap, or Grand Canyon National Monument whenever you see them, but pay no attention to the distances posted, which are wildly contradictory. Otherwise, just stay on what looks like the most-used road at each fork and maintain a southerly direction. There is a house near the point where a park ranger used to live, but it apparently hasn't been occupied in some time. The last 7 miles to the rim are bumpier. The informal campground is near the end of the road, a short walk from the tip of Toroweap Point.

Toroweap Point is the Grand Canyon's "back door," a wilderness area that hardly anyone sees. The last time I was there, on a Saturday afternoon in the middle of the tourist season, the only other visitors were a painter and a photographer. On weekdays you may find yourself completely alone on the canyon rim.

The rim here is lower than in the main part of the park. The approach to Toroweap Point is through a notch in the upper rim, so the point is actually on the hot, dry slickrock inner rim, the one you overlook from the North Rim, and about 100 miles downriver. The Colorado River is nearly 2,000 feet below you, between sheer cliffs. You can watch tiny-looking river rafts as they float past. The silence and the canyon's acoustics actually make it possible to eavesdrop on rafters' conversations. Toroweap Point also affords the only view of a major Grand Canyon formation, Vulcan's Throne.

When you leave Toroweap Point, instead of backtracking to rejoin the main itinerary at Fredonia, you can take a different unpaved road across the Arizona Strip to rejoin the main 22-day itinerary at St. George. The shortcut is 97 miles, all unpaved road, compared to 67 miles of unpaved road and 90 miles of highway. If you take the shortcut, you'll miss Zion National Park and save as much as an hour of driving time, depending on road conditions. To take this shortcut, backtrack 14 miles north from Toroweap Point, then take the road that forks to the left (west) to Mt. Trumbull. Twenty miles on, the road turns north. Stay on the same lonely road north for 63 more miles, and you'll suddenly come to St. George and I 15. Allow four to five hours for the drive.

Zion to Las Vegas

When early Mormon settler Isaac Behunin named this spectacular stretch of gorge Little Zion after the heavenly city of God, he was quite serious. "These great mountains," he declared, "are natural temples of God. We can worship here as well as in the man-made temples."

At first, when the area was declared a national monument in 1909, it was called Mukutuweap, the word used by the Paiute Indians who had considered it sacred ground. But this mouthful of a name stuck for only nine years. Zion became a national park in 1918, a year before the Grand Canyon did.

Suggested Schedule

8:30 a.m.	Breakfast at North Rim Lodge.
10:00 a.m.	Drive to Kanab.
Noon	Drive to Zion National Park.
1:00 p.m.	Explore Zion.
3:30 p.m.	Drive on to Interstate 15. You'll be back in Las Vegas in time for dinner.

Travel Route: Grand Canyon via Zion to Las Vegas (255 miles)

From the Grand Canyon North Rim, retrace your Day 14 route 75 miles north to Fredonia (where people returning from Toroweap Point rejoin the main route). Stay on US 89 for 17 more miles until you come to Mount Carmel Junction, then turn left on UT 9 to Zion National Park. Pay the $20 per vehicle fee. (Note for motorhomers: Any vehicle wider than 7'10" or higher than 11'4" must be escorted through the tunnel. There is a $10 fee for this. Vehicles over 19 feet long can't park in the Weeping Rock parking lot but should continue through the park to Springdale, then take the free shuttle back to the park visitors center.)

The steep entrance fee at Zion is designed to reduce the heavy sightseeing traffic that has clogged the park's scenic drive and parking areas in recent years. It's another good reason to have a National Parks Pass. (You can avoid the fee—and the park—by turning off to the west at Fredonia and following AZ 389, which becomes UT 59 at the state line and rejoins the road from Zion at Hurricane, 10 miles from Interstate 15.)

From the entrance to Zion, it's 51 miles westbound on UT 9, through the town of Hurricane, to St. George, southwestern Utah's largest city (pop. 12,000), where you will join I 15 southbound. A long, scenic descent through the Virgin River Gorge will drop you into the Mojave Desert, the lowest elevation and hottest place on this tour route. Thirteen miles south on the interstate, you will cross into Arizona briefly; 26 more miles will bring you to the Nevada state line. From there, it's a straight shot down I 15 to Las Vegas.

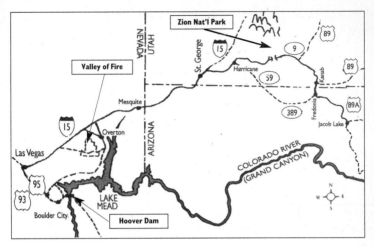

Zion to Las Vegas

Zion National Park

Zion is the quintessential scenic drive, a brief but intense burst of visual glory midway between the Grand Canyon and Las Vegas. The main road, with its long tunnel, tantalizing peekaboo windows, and sudden descent into Zion Canyon, by itself is marginally worth the high price of admission.

But people who don't get out of their cars can only catch a too-brief glimpse of Zion's beauty. Start with the short, easy walk to Weeping Rock from the parking area just past the main lodge. (For longer trails, see Hiking and Biking below.)

The Zion Canyon Scenic Drive turns off the main park road a short distance north of the visitors center and takes you up through Upper Zion Canyon. From April through October, this road is closed to private vehicles. Frequent shuttles carry people along this route, starting from the visitors center near the south entrance and making another pickup at Zion Lodge.

Passengers can get off a shuttle at any of several trailheads and points of interest, then catch a later shuttle to continue the tour. The shuttle is free; the catch is that there are not nearly enough parking spaces at the visitors center for the number of passengers the shuttles can accommodate. If you can't find parking there, continue out of the park to the small town of Springdale just outside the south entrance. There you'll find plenty of free parking and another free shuttle that takes you back to the visitors center.

Lodging and Food

For visitors who want to spend more time in Zion National Park, **Zion Lodge**, located near Weeping Rock, offers standard rooms, suites, and individual rustic cabins at rates ranging from $100 to $130 in summer, as low as $65 in winter. Make reservations well in advance by calling the lodge at (435) 586-7686 or the national parks reservation service AMFAC at (303) 297-2757. The lodge has a pleasantly old-fashioned dining room that serves very good, reasonably priced food.

You'll find dozens of other motels and restaurants in all price ranges in Springdale, just outside the park's south entrance.

Camping

Tent and RV sites are available at **Watchman Campground** and **South Campground**, (800) 365-2267, both located near the south entrance. Reservations are essential from April to October. On the Internet, go to reservations.nps.gov.

Hiking and Biking

The **Pa'rus Trail** runs through lower Zion Canyon between the visitors center and the lodge. This paved, wheelchair-accessible trail provides a car-free alternative that lets you see the canyon on foot or by bike.

Most of Zion National Park can't be reached, or even seen, by road. The park has 65 miles of trails, and maps are available at the visitors center. Though most Zion backcountry can only be reached on overnight hikes, any of the following trails makes a reasonable half-day or less hike: the **Emerald Pools Trail** starting at Zion Lodge, 1.2 miles round-trip; the **Hidden Canyon Trail** starting from the Weeping Rock parking area, 2 miles round-trip; the **Gateway to the Narrows Trail** starting at the Temple of Sinawava at the end of the Scenic Drive shuttle route, 2 miles round-trip; the **Canyon Overlook Trail** starting from the tunnel overlook parking area, 1 mile, steep; or the **Watchman Viewpoint Trail** starting at the south campground, 2 miles round-trip, steep. Carry plenty of water!

Walk in Beauty

I'll leave you now, as you head back down the interstate to Las Vegas. I sincerely hope you've enjoyed your southwestern trip as much as I've enjoyed sharing this information with you. I welcome your comments, suggestions, or discoveries. Write me c/o RDR Books, whose address appears on the copyright page of this book, or e-mail me directly at RichardKHarris@earthlink.net.

Travel beckons us with pretty places and enchanting promises but leaves us, at the end, with experiences that can translate into a better understanding of our world. As you finish your southwestern trip, take a moment to think back on the meaning of what you've seen. Nobody has said it better than the singer of "Nahasdzaan Shima," the Navajo Blessing Way chant:

> *Earth My Mother,*
> *We see you dressed in beautiful colors.*
> *Father Sky provides beautiful things to you.*
> *Like a man gives beautiful things to his wife.*
> *Now we use up and destroy these beautiful things.*
> *Now we are hurt because you are hurt.*
> *You only ask us for blessings and respect;*
> *You only expect us to work together in balance and*
> *   harmony.*
> *Earth My Mother,*
> *We will return to you these gifts of beauty and grace.*
> *We will return with beauty and grace.*

Index

About the Author

Richard Harris has written or co-written 27 other guide-books to the western United States, Mexico, Central America and the Caribbean for Ulysses Press, John Muir Publications, John Wiley & Sons, and Globe-Pequot Press. He has also served as contributing editor on guides to Mexico, New Mexico and other ports of call for Fodor's, Birnbaum, and Access guides. He is president of the New Mexico Book Association and a director and past president of PEN New Mexico. When not traveling, Richard writes and lives in Santa Fe, New Mexico.

I Should Have Stayed Home

The Worst Trips of Great Writers

Edited by ROGER RAPOPORT AND MARGUERITA CASTANERA

In this hilarious anthology, 50 top travel writers, novelists and journalists, including **Isabel Allende, Jan Morris**, **Barbara Kingsolver**, **Paul Theroux**, **Mary Morris**, **Dominique Lapierre**, **Eric Hansen**, **Rick Steves**, **Tony Wheeler** and **Helen Gurley Brown**, tell the stories of their greatest travel disasters. Most of the writers of these original essays are contributing their royalties to Oxfam America, the international relief organization. Guaranteed to whet your appetite or make you cancel your reservations.

ISBN: 1-57143-014-8

$17.95 (CAN. $21.95)
PAPERBACK
256 PAGES

I've Been Gone Far Too Long

Scientists' Worst Trips

Edited by MONIQUE BORGERHOFF-MULDER *and* WENDY LOGSDON

Here are the stories of 26 research scientists who go off the deep ends of the earth. Travel with a young researcher in Dian Fossey's camp as she is handed a gun and told to go out and shoot a gorilla poacher. See how a scientist reacts when he discovers a poisonous bushmaster in his bidet. From bush pilots and endangered species to Land Rover nightmares, this hair-raising book will keep you up past dawn. This book is a tribute to the courage of an intrepid band of researchers who have risked all to bring home the truth.

ISBN: 1-57143-054-7

$15.95 ($21.95 Can)
TRADE PAPERBACK
296 PAGES

After the Death of a Salesman

Business Trips to Hell

By ROGER RAPOPORT

In this sequel to bestselling *I Should Have Stayed Home* and *I've Been Gone Far Too Long,* business people tell of their greatest travel disasters—from the emergency room to the paddy wagon. Read this book and you'll be happy you weren't traveling with: oilman Jack Howard, cruise scout Marcia Wick, bookseller Monica Holmes, conductor Murray Gross, investor Jack Branagh, or publisher Cynthia Frank. Dedicated to the memory of Willy Loman, this tribute to corporate road warriors offers an amusing view of everything they don't want you to know in business school.

ISBN: 1-57143-062-8

$15.95 ($21.95 Can)
TRADE PAPERBACK
224 PAGES

I Really Should Have Stayed Home

Worst Journeys from Harare to Eternity

Edited by ROGER RAPOPORT AND Bob Drews

This collection of travel disasters is guaranteed to make you rethink those vacation plans. Before you pack your bags consider some of the many ways that the trip of a lifetime can bring you all the joy of a life sentence. In this outrageously funny anthology of vacation horror stories you'll spend one too many nights in Tunisia and flee nightmarish holidays that stretch from Harare to Eternity. This book is guaranteed to make you unfasten your seatbelt for the belly laugh of the travel season as you are trying to figure out why your wallet disappeared.

ISBN: 1-57143-081-4

$17.95 (CAN. $21.95)
Trade Paperback
200 Pages

THE GETAWAY GUIDES

Each of these guides is an ideal itinerary planner for short or long trips. Organized with daily trip schedules, each book gently guides you to well-known and off-the-beaten-track destinations with helpful directions, recommended schedules and convenient lodging and dining recommendations. Written by experts who visit every one of the places they recommend, the Getaway Guides can be used for long weekends, week-long trips or grand three-week tours. Perfect for budget travelers and those who prefer luxury, each Getaway Guide is years in the making to insure that your trip is a winner from beginning to end. Selective and fun to read, each book reveals the secrets travel writers usually reserve for their closest friends.

The Getaway Guide to Agatha Christie's England

By JUDITH HURDLE

ISBN 1-57143-071-7

$16.95 **($21.95 Can)**
TRADE PAPERBACK
192 PAGES

The Getaway Guide to California

By ROGER RAPOPORT

ISBN 1-57143-068-7

$17.95 **($21.95 Can)**
TRADE PAPERBACK
256 PAGES

The Getaway Guide to Washington

By RICHARD HARRIS

ISBN 1-57143-079-2

$17.95 **($21.95 Can)**
TRADE PAPERBACK
232 PAGES
JUNE 2002

The Getaway Guide to Colorado

By ROGER RAPOPORT

ISBN 1-57143-072-5

$17.95 **($21.95 Can)**
TRADE PAPERBACK
192 PAGES
JUNE 2002

Our books are available at your local bookstore, or contact RDR Books at 4456 Piedmont Avenue, Oakland, CA 94611. Phone (510) 595-0595. Fax (510) 595-0598.
Email: info@rdrbooks.com.
See our books on the Web at www.rdrbooks.com.